GREAT NIGHTS OF THE BIBLE

GREAT NIGHTS OF THE BIBLE

By

CLARENCE EDWARD MACARTNEY

ABINGDON PRESS

NEW YORK ● NASHVILLE

GREAT NIGHTS OF THE BIBLE

Library of Congress Catalog Card Number: 43-14422

PRINTED AND BOUND AT NASHVILLE,
TENNESSEE, UNITED STATES OF AMERICA

FOREWORD

IN THE BEGINNING WE READ THAT "GOD CALLED the light Day, and the darkness he called Night." If you listen to the voice of the night as it speaks to you in the pages of the Bible, you will hear many a deep word on life and destiny. In these sixteen sermons I have taken up what I believe to be the great outstanding nights of the Bible.

The history and the prophecy of these Old Testament and New Testament nights are full of instruction and of inspiration and hope for our souls. Here we shall meet men who by night found God and Eternal Life. Here we shall meet men who came to Christ by night, and men who fell away from him by night. Here we shall view the wreck and ruin of souls who sinned and lost their kingdoms in the night; and here, too, we shall listen to the stirring music of souls who, through prayer and faith in God, came off conquerors and more than conquerors in the night.

CLARENCE EDWARD MACARTNEY

CONTENTS

I

THE NIGHT OF DOOM

> "At midnight the Lord smote all the first-
> born in the land of Egypt."
>
> Exodus 12:29

UNTIL THE GREAT NIGHT UPON WHICH CHRIST
was born, and that other night when he was betrayed, this was the most momentous night in the
history of mankind. Some of God's mightiest acts
in the drama of providence and redemption have
taken place at night. This night opened a new
chapter in God's dealings with the world. When the
sun set that evening on Egyptian temple and palace
and river and field, Israel was a race of slaves,
hugging its chains. When the sun rose the next
morning, Israel was a nation, a nation on the march;
and ever since that nation has been on the march.
Egypt and all the great kingdoms of long ago have
disappeared, but Israel still lives. The Jew is eternal
because he follows the fiery pillar and cloudy path
of God's eternal purpose to redeem mankind.

Over all Egypt it is night. The April moon sheds
its golden light over all the land. Against the clear
sky rises the mighty Pyramid of Cheops, and in
front of that pyramid the Sphinx stares out over
the white moonlit desert with stony, mysterious, in-

scrutable gaze. By the banks of the winding Nile and the numerous canals, tall palm trees wave their branches in the soft evening air. Along the river a thousand villages are asleep. In his marble palace, flanked by porphyry columns wound with sculptured serpents and crowned with fierce eagles whose eyes flash with precious stones, Egypt's Pharaoh slumbers. In the temples of Isis and Osiris the fire has sunk on the altars and the priests and their attendants are asleep. In the huts and cottages of the peasants the sons of toil are deep in sleep, sore Labor's bath. In the dungeon the captive has forgotten the galling of his chains as sleep, balm of hurt minds, knits up his raveled sleeve of care. All Egypt is asleep.

The terrible plagues that have vexed the land; the hailstones that beat down their harvests; the frogs that came out of the waters into their houses; the diseases that smote their cattle and afflicted their own bodies; the blood that poisoned their fountains, crimsoned their waters; the locusts that clouded the sun; the thick darkness, the darkness that could be felt, which left them groping for light—all that is past. The enraged and obdurate Pharaoh has told Moses to see his face no more, and that if he comes again to the palace he will die. But with prophetic words the departing Moses had said to Pharaoh: "Thou hast spoken well, I will see thy face again no more." The nine plagues are past, but soon will come the sublime and awful climax of judgment.

Over all Egypt lies the mantle of night, broods the peace of slumber. But in the homes of the despised slaves, the Hebrews, all is different. Pass with me down this street in the Hebrew settlement. Here not a single Jew is to be seen, but on the door-posts and on the lintels of every slave's hut and home there is the stain of blood. Within the house every family stands by a table where a roasted lamb is ready to be eaten. Their staffs are in their hands, their loins girt about them, their shoes on their feet. Not a word is spoken, but in every countenance there is the look of expectation and of dread. If a careless child moves to open the door, immediately he is rebuked and restrained, for the command of God is, "None of you shall go out."

The hour of midnight approaches; and as it draws nigh, on every swart countenance there is the look of wonder and anticipation, from the octogenarian leaning on his staff to the little child in his mother's arms. Then at length it came—what they had been waiting for! Suddenly there arose a great cry, a long wail of woe, a tidal wave of lamentation that swept over the whole land. In his porphyry palace Pharaoh awoke with a sense of dread and called for his prince, only to learn that the prince of the realm, his first-born, was dead. Parents stirred uneasily and anxiously called for their stalwart sons, only to find that they were cold in death. Mothers awoke in terror to discover that the babes they clasped to their breasts were nothing but corpses. In the dungeon the prisoner shook his chains, and turned over to find that his son at his side was dead. In the temples of Isis and Osiris the priests called in vain upon the gods to restore their dead offspring. And in the fields even the cattle moaned over their dead; for that night the Angel of the Lord smote the first-born of Egypt, "from the first-born of Pharaoh that sat on his throne unto the firstborn of the captive that was in the dungeon; and all the firstborn of the cattle." Death reigned! Death! Death! Death! Death in the palace! Death in the cottage! Death in the temple! Death in the dungeon! Death on the river! Death on the highway! Death in the fields! Death! Death! Death! And everywhere a moan of anguish went up to Egypt's skies.

But in the houses of Israel, where, according to the commandment, the blood of the slain lamb had been sprinkled on the doorposts and on the lintels, there was no death. The Angel of Death passed over those homes. The frantic Pharaoh, feeling himself in the grip of Omnipotence and retribution, called for Moses and Aaron, and said to them:

"Rise up, and get you forth from among my people, both ye and the children of Israel; and go, serve the Lord, as ye have said." That night Israel was on the march. A nation had been emancipated. After four hundred years of bondage, the hour of deliverance had struck. Israel, the incarnation of God's plan and purpose, was on the march—a march that will never end until the world has been redeemed.

RETRIBUTION

Across the dark sky of that night of judgment and doom, when Egypt was smitten and Israel was delivered, is written one of God's great words—"Retribution." One of the cruel Pharaohs, seeking to thwart the ongoing purpose of God, had issued his infamous decree for the slaughter of the male children who should be born to the Jews. Every son was to be cast into the river Nile. In thousands of homes in Israel there was sorrow and lamentation when the first-born son was cruelly carried away by the guards of Pharaoh and cast into the river. But God was not sleeping. Behind the shadow of that great affliction he was keeping watch above his own. Now, when the cup of Egypt's iniquity is full, God judges that kingdom; and throughout the length and breadth of the land, on this dread night of Israel's deliverance, a cry of anguish arose, for the first-born in every home in Egypt lay dead. God not only punishes, but ofttimes he punishes in kind. In his *History of the French Revolution,* Thomas Carlyle tells of a minister of the Crown, Foulon, who, when someone asked in connection with one of the decrees of the Crown, "What will the people do?" exclaimed, "Let the people eat grass!" When the Bastille fell, the mob did not forget the cruel gibe of that minister of the king, "Let the people eat grass!" He was hung from a post, "and his mouth after death was filled with grass, amid sounds as of Tophet from a grass-eating people. Surely, if revenge is a kind of justice, it is a wild kind. They that would make grass to be eaten, do they now eat grass in this manner? After long-dumb, groaning generations, has the turn suddenly become theirs?"

The great Russian writer Maxim Gorky states the fact of judgment and retribution in this way: "Life has its wisdom. Its name is Accident. Sometimes it rewards us, but more often it takes revenge on us; and just as the sun endows each object with a shadow, so the wisdom of life prepares retribution for man's every act. This is true, this is inevitable, and we must all know and remember it."

GOD'S INVINCIBLE PLAN

Another truth which shines like a star in the darkness of that night of doom and deliverance in Egypt is that God's purpose is invincible. Egypt, which in the beginning had saved Israel from extinction, was not able now to destroy that people or thwart the purpose of God. After the Egyptian pause and delay of several centuries—for God is never in a hurry—his plan and purpose for humanity in the chosen people marched on to its goal. When the hour is darkest, and all things seem to conspire against the Truth—yes, in such a dreadful hour as this is today, with a wave of blood and carnage and violence and blasphemy sweeping over the world —God knows how to save his people and carry on his plan to its divine consummation. To every raging sea of destruction and of unbelief he is able to say, "Hitherto shalt thou come, but no further: and here shall thy proud waves be stayed."

CHRIST OUR SACRIFICE FOR SIN

But the one great truth that is proclaimed for us in this memorable night in Egypt when God smote the first-born, but delivered his people wherever the blood was sprinkled on the lintels, is that Christ bore our sins upon the Cross and died for us, and that by his death we live.

Fourteen hundred years have elapsed since the Israelites stood that night in their homes, with their loins girt and their staffs in their hands, waiting for the dreadful signal, the cry of smitten Egypt, which would send them forth on their march to freedom. Through all those fourteen centuries that memorable night has been commemorated in Israel by the feast of the Passover, the name of the feast being taken from the fact that on that night the destroying angel who smote the first-born of Egypt passed over the houses of Israel where the blood was sprinkled on the doorposts. Now, on this night, the disciples come to Jesus and ask him, "Where wilt thou that we prepare for thee to eat the passover?" When the arrangements have been made and the upper chamber prepared, Jesus sits down with his disciples to eat the Passover. As they are eating this feast, this Passover lamb, their minds running back to the great deliverance that God wrought for his people on that night through the blood of the lamb that was sprinkled over their doorposts, Jesus institutes a new feast which will be commemorated until the end of time, and will be the theme of the angels and the redeemed through all eternity. He broke the bread and said, "This is my body, which is broken for you," and poured out the cup and said, "This cup is the New Testament in my blood, which is shed for many for the remission of sins: drink ye all of it."

What was the meaning of that? The meaning of that is the heart of the Gospel, that is, that Christ is the Lamb of God slain from the foundations of the world. That was what John meant when he said that Christ was the Lamb of God which taketh away the sins of the world. That was what Paul meant when he said that Christ our Passover is sacrificed for us. That was what Isaiah meant when he said that He was wounded for our transgressions and bruised for our iniquities, and by his stripes we are healed.

This is the heart of the Gospel! This is the glory of it and the power of it! That Christ died as a young man, that he was cruelly betrayed by one of his disciples and denied by another and wickedly done to his death on the Cross by the Jews and the Romans—in all that, however touching and moving it might be, there is no Gospel, no saving power. But there is a Gospel and a Gospel of glory and power in the fact that Christ died for me, as my substitute. Paul said that it was this truth, that Christ died for our sins according to the Scriptures, that he delivered first of all when he preached to man. It is the first and the pre-eminent truth of Christianity; and one sign of that is that it is the most struck at by the enemies of Christ and of Christianity, for it is the most humbling, although the most uplifting, of all the truths of the Christian faith. An instance of the natural enmity of man to this central, sublime, and unique fact of the Christian faith is found in a recent statement by George Bernard Shaw, curiously enough, printed in the magazine of one of the English churches. The article attacks the Book of Common Prayer of the English Church. The chief of his objections to that book is that it is "saturated with the ancient, and to me quite infernal, superstition of atonement by blood sacrifice, which I believe Christianity must completely get rid of, if it is to survive among thoughtful people. Neither the Carthaginians nor the Mexicans ever, so far as I know, gave as a reason to propitiate their Deity, that God so loved the world that he had to be propitiated in this horrible way."

But repugnant as the truth may be to the heart of Bernard Shaw and to the heart of many another today, that is the very secret of the survival of Christianity. Instead of being the truth which Christianity is to get rid of if it is to survive, the sacrificial Cross of Christ is the secret of Christianity's survival through all the ages and the hope of its victory in the ages to come. It has something more than example; it has something more than ethics. It has a mighty Act of God's justice and love upon which you can put your trust.

In Westminster Abbey you will see a memorial tablet erected by the British Government in memory of Major John André, with whom Benedict Arnold negotiated for the surrender of the fortress of West Point, and who was hanged as a spy at Tappan on

October 2, 1780. It was a case where the man who ought to have been hanged escaped, and the man who was more unfortunate than criminal was hung. André, still in his twenties, was a gifted writer. Shortly before his execution he wrote a poem, "Hail, Sovereign Love," in which the great truth of the Atonement, of Christ's substitution for the sinner, is beautifully set forth. He describes how his soul was for a time too proud to seek a hiding place and despised the mention of the grace of God and how, fond of darkness more than light, he madly ran his sinful race without a hiding place. But when the arrows of distress and conviction began to pierce him, he found that he had no hiding place. He flew for refuge to Sinai on its fiery mount, to the law.

But Justice cried, with frowning face:
"This mountain is no Hiding Place."

But ere long mercy's angel appeared and led him,

at a placid pace,
To Jesus as a Hiding Place.

On Him almighty vengeance fell
Which must have sunk a world to Hell.
He bore it for a sinful race,
And thus became their Hiding Place.

Should sevenfold storms of thunder roll,
And shake this globe from pole to pole,

No thunderbolt shall daunt my face,
For Jesus is my Hiding Place.

A few more rolling suns at most
Shall land me on fair Canaan's coast,
When I shall sing the song of grace,
And see my glorious Hiding Place.

At one of the churches of New England, a devout
and believing visitor was amazed to hear the minister
say that instead of the bread and wine, for it was
the Communion Sabbath, he would distribute the
flowers of the season to his congregation! The idea
of Atonement, of substitution, of the Broken Body
and the shed Blood of our Lord, was repugnant to
him. Hence, he gave the congregation flowers instead of the sacred elements! A sad picture that is;
and all the more so because it is a picture of how
in many places the sublime central, inspiring, and
creative fact that Christ died for us has been passed
over, and in its place the people have been given
flowers and fancy and rhetoric. But there is no
substitute for Christ and him crucified, no substitute for that rugged and blood-stained Cross. Christ
reigns, as the hymn says, "throned upon the awful
Tree."

During the last year of the Civil War, a man
paid a visit to the battlefield of Chickamauga, where,
on September 19-20, 1863, the army under Rose-

crans was almost destroyed and was driven back into Chattanooga by the Confederate army under General Bragg. The battlefield was not then, as now, a beautiful and sacramental place, with stately monuments rising amid the trees, but still bore the scars of battle and was furrowed with recent graves. Over one of these new-made graves the visitor saw a man on his knees planting flowers. Walking over toward him he said in a kindly voice, "Is it a son who is buried there?" "No," the man answered. "An uncle, then, I suppose, or perhaps a brother? At least some relation?" "No," the man again replied. The visitor then said, "May I ask, then, whose memory it is that you cherish and thus honor?" Then the man told why he was there to decorate that grave. He had been drafted into the Confederate army, and no substitute, as the custom then was, could be procured. Just before he was to say good-by to his wife and his family and report to the training camp, a young man came to see him and said, "You have a wife and a family depending upon you. When you are gone you cannot support them, whereas I am unmarried, and have no one depending upon me. Let me go in your place." The offer was accepted and the young man went off in his place to the training camp. At the battle of Chickamauga he was mortally wounded.

The news of his death drifted back to the Southern home of the man whose place he had taken. As soon as he could save sufficient money he made the journey to Chickamauga and, after a search, found the grave of his friend with its rude marker.

The visitor, much touched by the narrative, went on his way over the battlefield; but coming back he passed this grave again. It was now well covered with flowers, but on a rough board at the head of the grave were cut these four words: "He died for me."

Those four words sound the length and the breadth and the depth and the height, the pathos, power, and glory of the Christian faith—"He died for me."

One of the notable paintings of Christ the Messiah is that by the German artist, Sternberg. This is the way the picture came to be painted. Meeting on the street a little gypsy girl, and being struck with her charm and beauty, he asked her to go with him to his studio that he might paint her. As she was sitting for him, she noticed on the wall a half-finished portrait of Christ on the Cross. The ignorant gypsy girl asked who it was. When told she said, "He must have been a very wicked man to have been nailed to a cross." The painter told her that on the contrary Christ was the best man that ever lived, and that he died on the Cross that others might live. "Did he die for you?" asked the simple and innocent child. That question, "Did he die for you?" touched the heart and the conscience of the painter, who was not himself a Christian. The question so weighed on his mind and so haunted him day and night, reminding him that Christ had died for him, that at length he himself accepted the sacrifice of Christ on the Cross and became a Christian man.

That is the question I leave with you. "Did he die for you?" Were you there when they crucified your Lord?

II

THE NIGHT OF DISSIPATION

> "In that night was Belshazzar the king of the Chaldeans slain."
>
> DANIEL 5:30

MIDNIGHT ON THE ST. LAWRENCE RIVER. IN THE darkness, barge after barge loaded with British soldiers floats silently down the broad river. As they near their destination, the commander of the army is reciting to the officers of his staff these lines:

> The curfew tolls the knell of parting day,
>   The lowing herd winds slowly o'er the lea,
> The ploughman homeward plods his weary way,
>   And leaves the world to darkness and to me.[1]

When he had finished the stanzas, he told his officers he would rather have been the author of that poem than win the battle with the French on the morrow. By a mountain path the army made its ascent in the darkness from the river to the Plains of Abraham. When the sun began to shine that morning on September 12, 1757, its rays were reflected upon the bayonets and cannon of the English army. The French army fought well and courageously all

[1] From "Elegy in a Country Churchyard," by Thomas Gray.

that day; but their courage and their heroism, and that of their gallant commander, Montcalm, were all in vain. The battle had been irrevocably lost by night. An empire, a kingdom, the dominion of North America, had been lost by night. It was not the first, and not the last, time that a battle and kingdom were lost by night.

"In that night was Belshazzar the king of the Chaldeans slain." What a night it was! In the East the day is fierce and its light garish, but the nights are full of wistful beauty and haunting mystery. The day has passed; and now night comes down over the great brown capital of Babylon, with its two hundred and fifty towers, and the tawny Euphrates flowing through it, washing the walls of palaces, orchards, and temples. The evening wind begins to stir. It shakes the leaves and flowers of the Hanging Gardens, built by Nebuchadnezzar for his bride, homesick on the flat Mesopotamian plains for the mountains of her native land. As if with an unseen censer, the wind, stealing over the city, scatters everywhere the fragrant incense of fruit and flower.

Now lights begin to glow in Belshazzar's palace, for this night there is to be a great banquet for Belshazzar and a thousand of his lords and nobles, their ladies, and his wives and concubines. From the windows of the yellow palace gorgeous golden banners float softly in the evening breeze. The banqueting hall is in keeping with the splendor of a world kingdom. The floor is of tessellated marble, white, red, black, and blue; and the walls are hung with tapestries on which are traced the winged symbols of Babylonish power and superstition. Green, yellow, and white curtains entwine the marble pillars, and Persian rugs with their mystic designs are spread out on the floor to deaden the tread of the banqueters. Candelabras, wrought in far-off Damascus, swing from the ceilings with their illumination, and golden candlesticks glow with soft radiance on the tables. At the windows are iron-girt balconies, where the guests can lean over the rail and look down upon the broad and darkly flowing Euphrates. In the center of the hall gushing fountains fling up their silver spray, while strange fish flash in the waters, and rare birds sing their songs in the cages along the walls. Innumerable braziers with pleasant intoxication fill the hall with sweet incense.

Now the guests are arriving. Arabian steeds, champing their bits, bring the chariots of the satraps, nobles and princes to the gates of the palace, where slaves and eunuchs clear the way for them as they pass up the grand stairway into the banqueting hall and take their places on gold and silver couches covered with crimson hangings. From the minstrels' gallery in one corner of the hall come the wanton strains of the flute, the cornet, the dulcimer, and the harp. When the guests have all been seated, the young monarch, Belshazzar, comes in with his wives and concubines and seats himself at the elevated table. Then the banquet commences. Every part of the realm has been ransacked for a contribution to that feast. When the feast is well under way, and Belshazzar and his nobles are heated with the wine of all nations, then the dancing women from the Caucasus and from Syria come in, and in their filmy garments glide wantonly in and out among the tables of the drunken nobles. Their immodest performance is greeted with shouts of applause from Belshazzar and all the drunken crew.

His head swimming with the wine, the young monarch resolves to startle his guests with an unheard-of performance. Nebuchadnezzar, when he took Jerusalem, had removed from the temple of God the golden vessels and carried them with him down to Babylon. These sacred vessels Belshazzar orders his attendants to bring in to the tables, so that he and his lords may drink the wine from them. The proposal is greeted with shouts of hilarious laughter; and the vessels which once had been borne by priestly hands in the service of Jehovah's temple are now brought in to Babylon's banquet and filled with the wine, and soon are smeared with the slaver of Belshazzar's drunken satraps as they sing the praises of the gods of Babylon, the gods of gold, silver, iron, brass, wood, and of stone. What a grand defiance! What a royal joke, to drink to the health of the heathen gods—the gods of silver, gold, iron, brass, wood, and stone—with the vessels dedicated to the worship of the most high God! Where now is the God of the Hebrews? Palsied be every tongue that will not sing the praises of Belshazzar and his gods, that will not cry, "O king, live forever!"

> The King was on his throne,
>   The Satraps thronged the hall;
> A thousand bright lamps shone
>   O'er that high festival.
> A thousand cups of gold,
>   In Judah deemed divine—
> Jehovah's vessels hold
>   The godless Heathen's wine.[2]

Where is the God of the Hebrews? He was nearer than anyone thought. Suddenly, just as he is about to put one of the sacred cups to his lips, Belshazzar hears a shout. He looks in the direction in which his cupbearer is pointing, and there, over against the candlestick, illuminated clearly by its sevenfold light, the king sees to his horror the fingers of a man's hand—not the whole hand or arm, only

---

[2] From "Vision of Belshazzar," by Lord Byron.

the fingers—and the fingers are writing on the wall.
When he sees the hand writing, the face of Belshazzar blanches; his slavering lips tremble; his knees
smite together in terror; and the holy vessel which
he holds in his defiling hand falls with a loud crash
on the marble pavement.

> In that same hour and hall,
>   The fingers of a hand
> Came forth against the wall,
>   And wrote as if on sand:
> The fingers of a man;—
>   A solitary hand
> Along the letters ran,
>   And traced them like a wand.[3]

Mene, Mene, Tekel, Upharsin! Those were the
words; but no one could read them. Belshazzar and
his nobles were too drunk to read them, even had
they been decipherable. Then the wise men, the
astrologers, and the soothsayers of Babylon were
brought in to see if they could make out these mysterious hieroglyphics. But all failed. Some tried
to read the words vertically, and some horizontally;
some from the left to the right, and some from the
right to the left. The writing was there, plain upon
the wall, but it was too much for the wisdom and
superstition of Babylon.

Then the queen remembered the old Hebrew

[3] *Ibid.*

statesman who had served under Nebuchadnezzar. The queen was not present at the banquet, for it was hardly a fit place for her. But when the news was brought to her of what had happened, she came in to encourage Belshazzar and told him of this Daniel, who was able to dissolve doubts, interpret dreams, and show hard sentences. The king then gave an order that Daniel should be brought in, and soon Daniel made his appearance. He was then about ninety years of age. What a contrast between this venerable Hebrew statesman and prophet and Belshazzar and his banqueters, as Daniel stood there with his white locks and his strong God-fearing countenance, surveying this spectacle of animalism, debauchery, and recent hilarity, now turned to terror and dismay!

How much trust God reposes in a faithful preacher of his word! Daniel might have pretended that he could not read the handwriting on the wall, any more than the wise men of Babylon. Or he might have given it a false, or a softer, meaning—something less, at least, than the sentence of judgment and doom. But Daniel was faithful to his God. Once when Bourdaloue was preaching before Louis XIV, wishing to rebuke the king for his profligate life, he drew in general terms the picture of a great sinner and the judgment which must fall upon him. But perceiving that the licentious monarch did not take the description and the warning to himself, Bourdaloue suddenly cried out in a voice of thunder, as Nathan once did to David, "Thou art the man!" Afterwards he said to the startled monarch, "Your majesty must not be angry, for in the pulpit I have no other master than the King of Kings."

This was the interpretation of the writing on the wall as declared by Daniel: "*Mene;* God hath numbered thy kingdom, and finished it." "*Tekel;* Thou art weighed in the balances, and art found wanting." "*Peres;* Thy kingdom is divided, and given to the Medes and Persians."

The words of doom were heard in awe and silence by Belshazzar and his lords. Then, suddenly, there was the loud blast of a trumpet, the sharp words of military command, and the rush of the feet of armed men as the soldiers of Darius, the general of Cyrus, charged up the grand stairway and burst into the banqueting hall. Swords flashed under the candelabras; groans, shouts, curses, pleas for mercy rang through the hall; and soon a thousand nobles and their women lay dead in the slush of mingled wine and blood, and among them lay Belshazzar.

That night they slew him on his father's throne,
He died unnoticed, and the hand unknown;
Crownless and sceptreless, Belshazzar lay,
A robe of purple round a form of clay.[4]

[4] From "The Feast of Belshazzar," by Lord Byron.

PROFANING THE HOLY

Belshazzar perished just at the time he was dese-crating and profaning the sacred vessels of the temple of Jehovah. Taking that in a figurative sense, all of us possess sacred vessels. Everyone is in a certain sense a king, and has within him that which is holy, and which ought not to be desecrated, pro-faned, or given to the dogs. That is the sad thing about every form of desecration: it profanes a sacred vessel. The body, Paul said, is the temple of the Holy Ghost, and whoever defiles that temple, God will destroy, just as he destroyed Belshazzar when he defiled the vessels of Jehovah's temple.

GOD'S WARNINGS

Belshazzar is an example of a man who refused to be taught and would not be warned; and now God mocks at his calamity. In that brief and powerful sermon, Daniel reminded the king of the pride and blasphemy of his predecessor upon the throne, Nebu-chadnezzar, and how God had driven him out to be wet with the dew of heaven, to eat grass like an ox, until his fingernails were like the talons of an eagle. Yet, unwarned by that, Belshazzar had gone Nebuchadnezzar one worse, and had exalted himself to a climax of infamy and blasphemy by drinking wine out of the cups of the Lord's House. "Though thou knewest all this, thou hast lifted up thyself

against the Lord of heaven." Neither Belshazzar
nor anyone else goes to his doom unwarned. There
are histories, ancient and modern; there are monuments to the curse of sin and to the judgments of
God all about us. Christ said of the city which
would not be saved, "If thou hadst known, ...
in this thy day, the things which belong unto thy
peace!" That was just the same as if he had said
what Daniel said, "Though thou knewest all this,"
for it is one thing to know, and another thing to act
upon that knowledge.

DRINK AND ITS VICTIMS

The doom of Belshazzar is a powerful sermon on
the use of strong drink. It was when he was in-
flamed with wine that Belshazzar committed his
abominable sacrilege and went down to his doom.
How many princely young men and young women,
too, have thrown away their kingdom, and have seen
a hand writing upon the wall in terms of woe and
retribution, of misery, shame, and sorrow unquench-
able, because they tarried long at the wine. "Who
hath woe? who hath sorrow? . . . . who hath wounds
without cause? who hath redness of eyes? They
that tarry long at the wine; they that go to seek
mixed wine."

Herodotus, the Greek historian, says that Cyrus
attacked and took Babylon at night, when the king

and the nobles were drunken. That was not the first nor the last kingdom to be lost when men were under the influence of strong drink. In contrast with Belshazzar is the story which Xenophon relates of this conqueror, young Cyrus. Cyrus as a youth was taught to shun the intoxicating cup. Once, on a visit to his royal grandfather in Media, Cyrus asked to be permitted to act as the cupbearer who served the wine to the king, after first tasting it himself. Cyrus did everything to perfection, and was loudly applauded by the nobles present, who were delighted with his perfect mimicry of the cupbearer, stepping so grandly and solemnly about. The king, too, praised him, but called his attention to one omission—he had neglected to taste the wine, as the cupbearer always did before he handed it to him. Cyrus said that the reason he had not tasted the wine was that he thought it had been poisoned. Asked why he imagined that, he answered, "It was poisoned the other day when you made a feast for your friends on your birthday. I knew by the effects. The things you do not allow us boys to do, you did yourself, for you were very rude and noisy. You could not even stand erect and steadily. So I thought that the wine which produced these effects must have been poisoned." There is a sermon on liquor and strong drink which is unanswerable in its simplicity and in its power.

KINGDOMS LOST BY NIGHT

Belshazzar lost his kingdom at night. He fell a victim to the sins of the night. Those who have kept the records tell us that more people die at night than die in the daytime. However that may be as to physical death, the death of the body, it is certainly true as to moral and spiritual death. More than one half the souls who go down to death and hell have been slain, like the king of Babylon, in the night. "In that night was Belshazzar the king of the Chaldeans slain!"

One night did the fatal business for this young king of Babylon. One night has done the fatal business for many another young man. In Philadelphia, some time ago, the courts had a peculiar case of a man who was adjudged sane by day but insane by night. That would seem to be true of not a few in the world about us today. Sometimes the mistakes and errors of the night suggest and demand the sins of the day. Lawless acts of the day are committed to cover up and meet the demands of the sins of the night. Night life has played its part, and a chief part, in the downfall of many a trusted employee. The stealings and dishonest transactions of the day are carried out to cover up the losses of the night. God knows there are enough sins by day; but many of them are the lineal descendants of the sins of the night. The true epitaph for many a

[35]

man who has made shipwreck of his career, and cast away his kingdom, and who now lies dissceptered and uncrowned, is this: "In that night he was slain." Every night, in every city, immortal souls, made for fellowship with God, made for the purple robe of honor and the scepter of right and the throne of influence, are stained, marred, broken, slain, lost. O night watchman! O policeman! O physician! O nurse! O priest! O minister! O magistrate! O father or mother! O sister or wife! what if thy lips could open and tell of the tragedies of the night!

WEIGHED IN THE BALANCE

Belshazzar suddenly, on that night, saw a hand writing on the wall. It was writing his judgment and doom, the last chapter in his history. Nothing now could be changed, nothing altered.

Weighed in the balance of his wives and concubines, and the thousand revelers at his banquet that night, Belshazzar was not found wanting. But it is not the judgment and balance of man that counts, but God's judgment and God's balance. Weighed in that balance, Belshazzar was found wanting.

What if the hand should now appear and write upon the wall of your palace, of your house, of your room? How would it find you? Would it find you wanting, or would it find you trusting? God weighs us in the balance. He is the Searcher of every thought, the Discerner of every secret desire, the Observer of every act. All of us, weighed in his balance, searched by his judgment, are found wanting. But God has provided for us a weight of righteousness which is not our own. Christ, Paul said, "having forgiven you all trespasses, blotting out the handwriting . . . . that was against us, ... took it out of the way, nailing it to his cross." When the hand begins to write, will it stop with that sentence, "Thou art weighed in the balances, and found wanting"? or will it add, but found trusting in Christ?

There is one character in the Bible whose portrait is painted always by night light. He appears just three times, and every time at night, and on his way to Jesus—Nicodemus. "The same came to Jesus by night." In the company of Christ you are safe.

O Jesus, keep me in thy sight,
And save me through the coming night.

III

THE NIGHT WITH WILD BEASTS

> "Then the king went to his palace, and
> passed the night fasting . . . . and his sleep
> went from him."
>
> DANIEL 6:18

"MOTHER, WHAT MAKES THE LIONS ROAR SO LOUDLY tonight?" The Babylonian mother clasped her child to her breast and answered: "Because for three days they have not been fed. The lions are famished; they are hungry. That is why they roar so loud."

All through the day those who live within a mile of the den of lions can hear the savage beasts roar. Mad with hunger, they pace restlessly up and down in their den, lashing their tawny hides with their tails, uncovering their cruel fangs and every now and then laying their jaw to the ground and emitting a frightful, earth-shaking roar. But at the eventide, when night has come down over Babylon and its hanging gardens, and the wind whispers among the willow trees along the banks of the broad Euphrates, there is silence in the den of lions. No longer do they roar.

"Mother, where are the lions? I do not hear them roaring now."

"No, child," answered the mother, "the lions have

been fed. That is why they do not roar. Now they are asleep."

Yes; now the lions were quiet. They had ceased to shake the earth with their roars; but not because they had partaken of food, for when food was offered them they had refused it. It was the first time the lions had ever refused to eat.

Over in his huge brown palace, where crimson banners float out of the windows that overlook the gardens smelling sweet of myrrh and cassia along the Euphrates, the king of all the world, Darius, is unable to sleep. Armed guards pace up and down the avenues before the gates of the palace and up and down the corridor in front of his royal chamber. The king lies upon a bed of ivory overlaid with gold, and his couch is soft with the softest wool of the Persian hills, and covered with the rarest silks and satins; yet the king cannot sleep. At length he arises, goes over to the open window—the window that looks toward the den of the lions—and listens intently for a moment. But all is silent. Not a sound of roaring now from the lions. Back to his couch Darius goes, only to toss for a few minutes, and then back again to the window. Back and forth, all through the night, the restless monarch paces, from the window to the couch, from the couch back to the window. At length, when the first ray of light streaks the eastern horizon, the king calls one of his officers, and leaving his chamber descends the marble stairway of the palace and makes his way to the gardens where the wild beasts are kept.

In that den of lions all is quiet and peaceful. Both man and beasts are asleep. The king could not sleep because his conscience smote him. But here, in a den of lions, a strange, strange spectacle. Their rage abated, there lie the huge beasts, stretched out in slumber; and with his head resting on the flank of one of the lions, his silver hair contrasting with the yellow hide of the beast, sleeps the man of God, the man who feared God more than he feared the beasts, the first lion tamer.

The story is perhaps the most familiar of all the stories of the Bible, and yet not too familiar to lose its grand and stirring meaning. To understand the great triumph of Daniel in the lions' den, we must recall the previous history of the man; for the boy, indeed, was father to the man. When we know the early life of Daniel, we understand how inevitable it was that he should have taken the stand he did when God gave him victory over Darius and his wild beasts.

A STAND FOR CONSCIENCE

When he came down with those other three Hebrew lads, the pick of the young men of Jerusalem, to be educated at the court of Nebuchadnezzar, Dan-

iel at the very start commenced his life in Babylon
by taking a stand for his God and for his religion.
The king changed his name from Daniel to Belte-
shazzar, as he had changed the names of the other
three young men. But he could not change the soul
of Daniel or make him forget the name of his God.
The first thing that confronted Daniel and his companions was the menu, the fare, at the king's table,
where was set before them wine that had been
offered to heathen gods, and flesh which the law of
Moses forbade them to eat.

What would Daniel do? What would he advise
his companions to do? The ordinary young man
would have said: "Jerusalem is fallen. God was not
able to protect his people there. Why should I serve
him here? I am a captive in Babylon. Here is to
be my life, my future career, my destiny. If I re-
fuse the food which the king sets before me, I shall
offend His Majesty, and my great future and my
chances for distinction in this kingdom will vanish.
Moreover, the main thing is what is in your heart
and in your soul, not the wine that you drink, not
the flesh that you eat. Here I am in Babylon, and in
Babylon I will do as the Babylonians do!"

But that was not what Daniel said. That was not
what Daniel did. Instead of that, Daniel purposed
in his heart that he would not defile himself with
the king's meat. There was no shaking him out of

that purpose. Without a purpose, without principles, without standards, no young man will count for anything in this world. The result of Daniel's stand was that he not only prospered and grew strong with the homely diet of water and pulse, but that he won the respect of the officers of the court and the king himself. That is always true. Men may pretend to laugh and sneer at the one who has standards, convictions, and holds to them. But in their heart of hearts they respect such a man. Daniel not only won the respect of the Babylonians, but we can be certain that the stand he took exerted a great influence upon those other young men, for he was evidently the leader of them. For some reason Daniel seems to have been exempted from that great trial, when his three companions were cast into the fiery furnace because they would not bow down to the golden image of Nebuchadnezzar. But when you read of their heroic stand, and how they said to the king that they believed that their God would deliver them, but if not, even if they burned to ashes, they would not bow down to that image or worship those gods; and how in the furnace they were unscorched in the flame; and how, when the king came to see what was left of them, he saw walking by their side the form of a fourth who was like unto the Son of Man—when you read all that, and your heart is stirred by it, it is well to remember that

the magnificent conduct of those Hebrew lads must
have been inspired by the stand of Daniel.

THE PLOT

Under several kings, and through successive
reigns, Daniel rose from honor to honor. He was
too valuable a man for the empire to lose, and in the
day of the great Darius he is the prime minister of
all that vast empire. But he was guilty of one
serious crime—the crime of success. No one ever
committed that crime without having someone on
his trail. Whether he be a statesman, a doctor, a
poet, a preacher, an inventor, an historian, or an
artist, when a man climbs to the heights he will
have to look down upon the scorn and envy and
jealousy of the world and of the men around him,
and beneath him. "He who climbs the mountain
slopes will find the loftiest peaks most clothed in
snow; and he who conquers or subdues mankind
must look down on the hate of men below." The
snowbird asked the snowflake why the snowflake did
not like it. "Because," answered the snowflake, "you
are going up, and I am going down." When one
man is going up, and others are slipping down, or
when they themselves cannot make the grade, you
can count on it that some of them will try to vent
their spleen and envy upon the man who is going up.
So the enemies of Daniel plotted for his downfall.

But the question was, How to get at him? How could they bring him low? Someone suggested that they charge him with dishonesty in his handling, as Chancellor of the Exchequer, the rich revenues of the kingdom. But all the others agreed that Daniel was an honest man. He had lived too long and served too faithfully under too many kings to be charged with dishonesty. Another suggested that they bring charges of treason against him, that they "frame" him, as it were, for treasonable negotiations with other kingdoms, or with dissatisfied provinces of the kingdom of Babylon. But all the rest agreed that that too would be futile. Daniel had too long a record of integrity and loyalty to the kings and the empires he had served to be charged with treason.

Then another came forward with his suggestion. It was this: "The only way in which we can find occasion against this Daniel will be in putting him into a position where his loyalty to the God of Israel will conflict with the laws of the kingdom of Babylon." "But," asked the others, "where can we find such a situation? All through his life, and under all the kings that he has served, Daniel has been able to be loyal to the God of Israel, and at the same time faithfully serve his master, the king. And for doing that he has won the respect of all the kings whom he has served." "Yes, that I know full well," answered the man who conceived the plot against Daniel; "but we shall persuade the king by flattery. We shall get him to sign a royal decree that for a period of thirty days no one shall ask a petition of any god or any man, save of the king. If he prays to any but the king, he shall be cast into the den of lions." "Splendid! The very thing!" the others all ejaculated.

Off they went to the royal palace, and with pleasing flattery induced the foolish king to issue and sign the decree. The decree was posted all over the walls of the palace and throughout the city, and loud-mouthed criers proclaimed it to the multitudes on Babylon's streets. "For thirty days none shall pray to any god or man but the king." Then they set watchers about the palace of Daniel to see what he would do. They had no doubts at all as to what he would do. Neither did Daniel have any doubt. As soon as Daniel heard that decree, what did he do? At the accustomed hour he opened his window northward and westward towards Jerusalem, the once Holy City, towards the Temple, "and prayed, and gave thanks before his God, as he did aforetime."

When I get through preaching the Bible I would like to paint it. And here is one of the great scenes of the Bible that I would like to paint—that aged, gray-haired saint of God kneeling down three times a day with the window opened towards Jerusalem. The wicked plotters were watching him, and with great satisfaction saw him make those prayers. But others were watching him also. The stars watched him by night; the sun watched him by day; the angels of heaven were watching him too. And God on his throne was watching him, and successive ages and generations of men who love and honor the truth, and men who stand for the truth, from age to age, all watched Daniel on his knees.

When the king heard how he had been trapped, and how he must now honor his own decree by casting Daniel into the lions' den, whom he honored and respected, and feared as a righteous man, he was sorry—and, more than that, he was sore afraid. Yet just as Herod, when he had been trapped by his foolish oath and by the wicked cunning of Herodias into a place where he had to go back on his word or commit a great crime, chose "for their sakes"—the sake of his nobles, and the sake of Herodias—to commit that crime, and beheaded John the Baptist, so Darius, trapped by his own decree, ordered Daniel cast into the den of lions.

THE POWER OF CONSCIENCE

In the morning Darius, who all the day before had labored to the going down of the sun to deliver Daniel, and all through the night had paced up and down in his chamber thinking about Daniel, hastened to the den of lions. How mighty, mysterious, and sublime a thing is the voice of God speaking in man's breast and through man's conscience! At first you say, how extraordinary a thing that this King Darius, master and despot of the world, should be troubled in mind about the fate of Daniel. In that vast empire, what was one man but an insect? It was within his power to order the execution of one of his subjects in any part of the world, and no doubt he had often done that and then sat down to a comfortable banquet and passed the night in peaceful, untroubled slumber. But on this occasion there was no sleep and no rest, and no peace in the heart of Darius. His conscience smote him because he had delivered a man of God, a righteous man, up to a cruel and shameful death. There is one of the great triumphs of conscience—that monarch of the world, distraught and uneasy, standing there in the first gray light of the morning, at the mouth of the den of lions, and calling down to Daniel, "O Daniel, servant of the living God, is thy God, whom thou servest continually, able to deliver thee from the lions?" And up from the den of lions came the answer, "O king, live for ever. My God hath sent his angel, and hath shut the lions' mouths, that they have not hurt me."

DANIEL LIVES FOREVER

Henceforth Daniel lives forever. His place among the immortals is secure. To all intents and purposes he had, without the least hesitation, offered up his life in loyalty to his faith and to his God. Greater love and greater courage hath no man than this, that a man should lay down his life for his soul. There is no substitute for the man of God. Organizations, schools of thought, theories, programs, institutions, combined activities, can never, never take the place of one true man of God. No wonder that, in the days of Ezekiel, God, speaking through the prophet Ezekiel, names Daniel as one of the three Old Testament characters, up to that age, who would have the most influence with God; for in pronouncing the doom of Jerusalem, God said that even if those three men—Noah, Job, and Daniel—dwelt in the city, even their presence could not stay the judgment.

Great is the influence of the godly man, and great is the reward of the godly man. God says in his word, "The secret of the Lord is with them that fear him." To this man who feared him, in visions of overwhelming glory, was revealed the future and was opened unto him the books of the world's to-morrow and the jurisprudence of the human race.

That was part of Daniel's reward. But more than that, Daniel was told that after the last great

[48]

judgments had fallen upon the world, and the history of mankind had been wound up, he would have his place; he would stand in his lot at the end of the days. To Daniel it was revealed, and of Daniel, too, God was speaking, that "they that be wise shall shine as the brightness of the firmament; and they that turn many to righteousness as the stars for ever and ever." Think of what it would be like, think of what the world would be like today, had there been no men like Daniel, and Elijah, and Isaiah, and Paul, and Luther, who stood nobly for God's truth, and "loved not their lives unto the death"! How true is this word, that these godly men, they that be wise, and they that turn many to righteousness, by their words and by their influence, shall shine as the brightness of the firmament and as the stars forever and ever!

LIONS NOT EXTINCT

Those lions that Daniel dared, and out of whose jaws he was delivered, are not extinct. What did Peter say? "Your adversary the devil, as a roaring lion, walketh about, seeking whom he may devour." No, they are not extinct. Still they prowl and still they roar. Still they roar for their prey. What are these lions but symbols of the obstacles, the trials and temptations and difficulties, which our souls must overcome? Each of us, in our private battling, in our private theater of trial, is put to the test, to see if we will stand by our convictions and our faith, or desert them and deny them. That is the great sermon, the great inspiration, of Daniel's life. He tells you how to dare, and how to stand, and how to overcome. When you do that, the same God who delivered him and made him a blessing unto other men, as the stars of the night bless the world, will deliver you and will make your life a blessing in your day and generation, and long after you, to your fellow men.

FORTY WRESTLERS

Have you ever heard of the Forty Wrestlers? The Forty Wrestlers were Christian soldiers in one of the legions of the Roman army. The army was on a campaign in the high mountains of Armenia in Asia Minor, and it was bitter winter. The emperor had issued a decree to the generals of all his armies that on a given day the soldiers must march past the statue of the emperor, do obeisance, and pour out a libation of wine and drop incense on the fire.

At the appointed time the trumpets blew and the army marched past the emperor's statue, where they bowed and poured out the wine and offered the incense, as if to a god. But the Forty Wrestlers, these Christian soldiers, refused to pay the emperor's statue divine honors. They were renowned for their prowess on the field of battle and for their triumphs in the amphitheaters and athletic games. Their general, who thought highly of them, besought them for his sake and their love for him to obey the decree. For a moment they hesitated, as they thought of the sweetness of life and their families at home—but it was only for a moment. Then they answered their general and said, "For Rome we will fight on any field and under any sky. In the service of the emperor, if necessary, we will die. But we worship no one save our Master, Jesus Christ." Then with great sorrow and reluctance the general pronounced the sentence of punishment decreed for those who refused to worship the image of the emperor. The forty soldiers were stripped of their armor which they had so honored in many a hard-fought campaign. Their helmets and breastplates and shields and spears and swords were taken from them. Then they were divested of their undergarments and their sandals, and, stark naked, were driven out in the sub-zero weather upon the frozen lake. The night had come down, and as the soldiers of the legion sat about the campfires in their bivouacs they could hear the voices of the Forty Wrestlers as they sang, "Forty Wrestlers wrestling for thee, O Christ, claim for thee the victory and from thee the Crown." As the night passed, their song grew fainter and fainter, as man after man succumbed to the cold and fell lifeless on the ice. At length only one survivor was left. Naked and trembling and shivering, he appeared before the tent of the general and said to the sentinel, "I will drop the incense and pour the wine." But the sentinel, who, although a pagan, had been moved by the heroic faith of the Forty Wrestlers, answered, "Since thou hast proved a coward, I will take thy place." With that he stripped off his armor and his clothing and went out in the night upon the ice to take his stand among the thirty-nine who had fallen. For a time the soldiers about the campfire heard his voice singing as he caught up the chant of those who had fallen: "Forty Wrestlers wrestling for thee, O Christ, claim for thee the victory and from thee the Crown." At length he too fell dead upon the ice. When the morning sun rose over the bleak Armenian mountains, that was what it looked down upon—the Forty Wrestlers who had died for Christ, and from whom they had received the Crown.

IV

Outlined ⁷⁄₈₀₀

THE NIGHT OF THE SHIPWRECK

"About midnight the shipmen deemed that
they drew near to some country."

Acts 27:27

BREAKERS AHEAD! BREAKERS AHEAD! BREAKERS
ahead!

That cry, which seamen dread above all others,
was the cry that went up at midnight from the helpless waterlogged ship that was driving toward the
rocky coast of Malta. After nineteen hundred years,
the Island of Malta has again been upon everyone's
lips as the most bombed area in all the world. Its
yellow soil and the beautiful blue waters which en-
circle it have been strewn with the wreckage of the
German and Italian planes which sought to blast it
into submission; but it still stands today, a bas-
tion of democracy and freedom.

A wreck is always a terrifying experience, whether
it be a train wreck, a carriage wreck, an automobile
wreck, or an airplane wreck. But most terrible of
all is a shipwreck, partly because of the prolonged
strain of agony under which shipwrecked people
suffer. This is the tale of a shipwreck, and one of
the greatest, perhaps the greatest, ever written. It
surpasses Victor Hugo's story of the wreck in *The*

[53]

Man Who Laughs, and Defoe's thrilling account of the wreck of Robinson Crusoe's ship, and James Fenimore Cooper's story of the wreck in *The Spy.*

A wreck by day is bad enough, but a wreck by night is worst of all. Even when the sea is comparatively calm, there is something about a dark night on the ocean which is full of dread and menace, and which makes one shrug the shoulders in fear as one leans over the rail of the steamer and listens to the sound of the black waters as they go swishing by the ship. But how terrible is the sea when there is a storm at night! It was midnight that this cry went up on Paul's ship. One night of a storm is bad enough, but this was a night which had lasted for two weeks—half a month. It was two weeks now since this large grain ship, tempted by the south soft winds, had set sail from the Harbor of Fair Havens, seeking to reach the port of Phenice, just a little farther along the south shore of Crete. But she had scarcely cleared the headlands when the winds shifted. Up near Mount Ida, the fabled abode of Zeus, Euroclydon, the terror of seamen, had been watching and waiting for his deluded victims. Now his hour had come, and he loosed upon them all his furies. When the hurricane broke over the ship and tossed it hither and yon like a cork, all they could do in the way of navigation was to let her run before the sea and the wind.

Day after day, night after night, with no light of
the sun by day and no light of the stars by night,
the ship plunged and wallowed in the great deep.
As the Psalmist put it in his splendid description of
a storm at sea, "They mount up to the heaven, they
go down again to the depths." Huddled on the deck,
clinging in terror to mast or spar or stanchion,
drenched with the waves and cut with the winds,
the two hundred and seventy-six souls on board
waited for what they felt—all but Paul and his two
companions—was certain death.

At length, after two weeks of drifting before the
wind in the raging seas, at midnight on the four-
teenth night a cry went up from the lookout, "Breakers ahead!" Luke says, "The shipmen deemed that
they drew near to some country." That was the
only way they could know it—by the ominous thunder of the breakers. Immediately the captain ordered the leadsman to sound. The first sounding
showed twenty fathoms; then in a few minutes fifteen fathoms. That let them know they were drifting rapidly on a dangerous lee shore. Putting his
trumpet to his lips and lifting his voice above the
roar of the gale, the captain shouted, "Stern anchors down!" Immediately the seamen let four
anchors down from the stern. The reason for that
is obvious. They were close now to the shore, and
if they had anchored from the bow, the ship would

have swung with the current and the wind and would have been that much nearer to the breakers. Hence, they anchored from the stern and "wished for the day."

Everything now depends upon those four anchors. If they drag, or if their cables snap, the ship will drive onto the rocks in the darkness and all will perish. But some nameless ironworker of Damascus has done his work well. Some ropemaker of Syracuse had done his work well. Some carpenter of Brundisium had been faithful and conscientious in his w k. When you do an honest piece of work, whether it is preparing a sermon, or weaving a garment, or forging an iron, or making a rope, you never know how many you will serve. The cables held; the anchors gripped the bottom and held the ship fast. All through the night those two hundred and seventy-six passengers waited and wished and prayed for the dawn. What a night it must have been—the sky as black as ink, the great waves sweeping now and then completely over the ship, as her stern, held by four anchors, went under, and her prow pointed toward the sky, until it seemed as if the ship would turn completely over. But at length the dawn came. Just in front of them they could see the huge gray cliffs, with the sea climbing over them.

I was there once, but it was a beautiful August

Sabbath day, and the cliffs looked almost friendly
with their black and gray relieved by a touch of
purple and green. Far below me was the little
bay—St. Paul's Bay, they call it now—with smooth
sandy beaches, and hardly a ripple on the blue sea
as it gently caressed the lower rocks; and out on an
island the heroic statue of St. Paul. How calm,
gentle, peaceful, innocent, and harmless thou art today, O Sea; as blue as the heaven above thee, as
deep as thought, as silent as time. For how many
ages hast thou rolled against these rocks. Where
are the fleets that once swept over thee? The ships
of Tarshish and of Tyre, the triremes of Carthage
and of Greece? The ships of the Venetian mer-
chants and the Moorish pirates, and the French and
English frigates? On thy calm azure face I read
as on a manuscript the long story of the struggle
for empire and dominion. Yet on this peaceful
Sabbath how calm and still thou art! Who could
imagine that for ages thou hast been the arena for
the display of man's passion and anger, or that thou
thyself, so quiet and harmless now, hast had thy
moods and moments of anger and destruction?

But it was different on that late autumn morning
when Paul and his companions looked shoreward
and saw the mighty cliffs rise out of the mists.

At length, as the light grew stronger, they were
able to make out a little inlet. The seamen cut

the cables to the anchors with their axes. The one sail they had left was hoisted, and the ship, driven with the wind and the current, leaped shoreward like an arrow from the bow. At first it looked as if she would get clear up on the beach; but some distance from the shore she grounded on the rocks and immediately began to break up. All the prisoners then were turned loose and the order was given for everyone to cast himself into the sea. Here they come— one on a board, with another on top of him; another clinging to a broken mast; another to a plank that had been loosened from the deck, and some swimming. Here they come, all of them, struggling up the beach out of the clutches of the angry sea. Ten, twenty, forty, fifty, seventy-five, one hundred, one hundred and fifty, two hundred, two hundred and fifty, two hundred and seventy-six! So the whole ship's company—centurion, supercargo, captain, soldiers, passengers, prisoners, Paul, Luke, Aristarchus—all escaped safe to the shore. Some by swimming, "some on boards, and some on broken pieces of the ship. And so it came to pass, that they escaped all safe to land."

Out of the storm and hurricane of that night, with its fears and despairs, its heroism and its faith, there are a number of truths which are of value to us who take this long and ofttimes dangerous voyage of life. It is a wonderful journey, this voyage of life, with wonderful lands to visit, great discoveries to be made; but there are treacherous tides and currents, dangerous sands and shoals, and cruel rocks and reefs. Now the beguiling Etesian south wind blows softly; then sometimes the howling, raging Euroclydon. The Holy Spirit has preserved for our instruction and comfort and warning the story of this shipwreck. Here are some of the things we can learn from it:

BEWARE OF THE SOFT WIND OF TEMPTATION

This ship on which Paul was traveling had already weathered one great storm on its journey from Syria towards Rome. To escape from the fury of the storm, the ship had taken refuge at the Harbor of Fair Havens, on the southern shore of the Island of Crete. A little farther along on the island was a much larger place—Phenice. The harbor was more commodious; the town was bigger; and there were amusements and diversions for the soldiers and sailors. So, when the storm had abated, when the northeast wind changed to the pleasant south wind, which blows so commonly in the Mediterranean, the centurion and the captain determined to sail for Phenice. "When the south wind blew softly," Luke says, "supposing that they had obtained their purpose, they weighed anchor and sailed along Crete." But they had hardly cleared the headlands at Fair

Havens till the storm broke upon them in all its fury. And now all that they could do was to cut away the tangled gear and broken masts that littered the deck after the first blast of the storm, throw overboard part of the cargo of grain, hoist a storm sail, and let the ship drive before the hurricane.

What happened to that ship is a parable of what often happens to the souls of men. Men are deceived and tempted and beguiled, and sometimes ruined, by the soft winds of pleasure and prosperity. The sea always whispers softly before it utters its curses and imprecations. The ancient method of temptation in its warfare against the soul, ever since the Tempter told the woman that the forbidden fruit of the Garden was good to look upon and good to taste, has been to speak first with the south wind and then smite with the hurricane. When, that day at the Harbor of Fair Havens, the south wind was gently filling the great sail of the vessel, and the blue waters, just stirred by the kiss of the wind, were rippling in the sunlight, nothing could have seemed further away than what happened within an hour— the rage of the hurricane—the ship strewn with the wreckage of broken masts and torn and tangled rigging, and the passengers, prisoners, and crew holding on for dear life to the side of the ship. So, when people are taking the first steps in evil and enjoying the first fruits of transgression, it does not seem possible that suffering and danger and death and judgment are waiting for them just beyond the horizon.

A man once designed a bejeweled goblet out of which wine was to be drunk. He who drank from the cup enjoyed the taste and the pleasing intoxication of the wine. But when he had reached the bottom, a coiled serpent suddenly struck out with its dripping fangs. So is it always with temptation and sin. Beware of the south wind! Beware of the end! The locusts of the Apocalypse which swarmed out of the abyss had crowns of gold on their heads, but their stings were in their tails. Beware of the end. "There is a way which seemeth right unto a man, but the end thereof are the ways of death."

ANCHORS FOR THE SOUL

As soon as the seamen on watch that night heard the roar of the breakers as they smashed against the great cliffs of Malta, they knew that the ship was in great danger, and immediately after taking soundings the captain ordered the seamen to let go four anchors from the stern of the vessel. The plight that the ship was now in, and the dreadful experience of the past two weeks, were due to the fact that hitherto they had disregarded the warnings which they had received. They had already passed through one severe storm before this storm broke over them, and only with the greatest difficulty and labor had been able to take refuge in the port of Fair Havens. That ought to have warned them. In addition to that, when they were proposing to set sail again Paul had warned them that the voyage would be one of great danger, and that they would be sure to encounter hurricanes. But the desire for ease and for pleasure deceived them into disregarding those warnings, and they set sail on the disastrous voyage which now was coming to an end on the rocks at Malta.

God gives the soul plenty of warnings. There are public warnings from God's Word, like this sermon. There are private warnings that come from earnest friends and those who love you and pray for you. There are the warnings which come from the experience of others who have made shipwreck on the sea of life. There are warnings and premonitions which rise out of a man's own conscience, when the still small voice of God tells him to beware. Always these danger signals are flashing in our own lives and in the lives of other men, letting us know when we draw near to some dangerous shore, inviting us to Stop! Look! Listen! What flaming lessons, what stern and earnest teachers! Everywhere we see men and women getting ensnared, entangled, soiled, defiled, broken, and wrecked on the sea of life. O Life, what a teacher thou art! How generous with thy lessons, how patient with thy unwilling scholars, how plain thy instruction, how eloquent thy pleading, and how sad thy farewell to the soul that would not be warned!

But this time when the seamen received the warning, when they heard the crash of the breakers against Malta's rocks, they acted promptly and acted wisely. They let go four anchors out of the stern, and those anchors saved the ship and saved the life of everyone on board. Everything depended that night on those four anchors. The masts were gone; the sails were gone; the rigging was gone. The only thing left on that ship was its anchors.

On the voyage of life the soul needs an anchor. No one in his senses would go to sea, even in the most modern of vessels, if, on walking up the gangplank, he should see this notice: "Passengers, please take note: This vessel carries no anchors." No one, I say, would sail on such a ship. The anchor on a ship today, although everything else has changed about the ships that sail the seven seas, is much the same in shape and in operation as those anchors which they cast out of the stern that night from that ship driving on the rocks of Malta. So human life changes outwardly, but not inwardly. We have automobiles, radios, airships, and all the devices of our modern civilization. But inwardly life is much the same—the same perils, the same sorrows, the same temptations. The soul of man still needs the anchor on its voyage across life's treacherous sea.

Here are four anchors which all of us would do well to carry with us on the voyage of life: One is the anchor of a relationship to the church, and the habit of worship in the house of God. Of the noblest Young Man that ever lived it was written that "as his custom was, he went into the synagogue [the church of his day] on the sabbath day." Young men who wish to rise to the highest will follow in his steps. The House of God is a defense against temptation. On the towers of many of the churches you will see gargoyles, hideous-looking creatures, glaring down at the street. The symbolism of the gargoyle seems to express the idea that an evil spirit is being driven out of the heart of the worshiper. What a story it would be if we could tell of all those who have found peace and hope and warning and cleansing and guidance in the worship of God's house.

What evil spirits have been cast out, what temptations conquered, what passions subdued, what noble goals seen, what destinies chosen, and what decisions made in the house of God which shall bless the soul as long as the moon and the stars endure! How many there are today who can rise up and say with all the depth of their being, "I was glad when they said unto me, Let us go into the house of the Lord."

A second anchor that will not drag in the time of storm is the anchor of home ties and affections. A British admiral used to say that he never knew a midshipman to make a failure of his profession who had kept up the habit of writing a weekly letter to his home. In his story of the temptation of Joseph, the German author, Thomas Mann, says that when Joseph was about to yield to the fierce temptation of Potiphar's wife, suddenly he saw the face of his father Jacob, and that made him think of Jacob's God, and that in turn held him back from temptation, so that he was able to cry out, "How then can I do this great wickedness, and sin against God?" The thought of a godly home and a godly father and mother has often risen up as a barrier which has held back the soul from the abyss of temptation and sin.

The third anchor for the soul is the Bible. A poll was recently taken of the men in the navy, asking what books they would like to have. More than fifty per cent selected the Bible. These men realize that they are going into places of danger, of suffering, and of possible death, and for such a place and such an hour there is only one Book, and that is the Bible. If you use it, it will keep you from drifting upon dangerous shores, and it will be your friend and helper in every time of danger and distress. The father of one of our heroic marines who had passed through some of the fierce battles in the South Seas said that he was confident that his son would survive the vicissitudes of battle because he carried a Bible under his uniform. The Civil War had many stories of men who carried their Bibles in their blouses over their hearts and were saved from death because the bullet lodged in the Bible. That sometimes might happen, and again it might not happen. The bullet might go clear through the soldier's Bible and pierce his heart. But, figuratively speaking, there is no question about the protection for the soul that the Bible gives. In the battle of life the truth of the Bible applied to daily life will defend the soul. It is a shield that stops the bullet of the tempter; it is an anchor which will not drag.

A fourth anchor is the anchor of prayer. In the Greek Navy they had what they called the sacred anchor, the strongest anchor in the ship, the last reserve, to be used only in emergency. Prayer is like that. It is our strongest, most sacred anchor; only, unlike that sacred anchor of the Greeks, it is to be used all the time. The prophets, the apostles, the martyrs, Peter, Paul, and Christ, your fathers and mothers, they all used this sacred anchor and it never failed them. Keep in touch with heaven by

prayer. Defend your soul from Satan by prayer.
I have known men who fell into sin and drifted
away from God when they stopped praying; but I
have never yet heard of a man who fell into sin on
his knees.

CONCLUSION

The last lesson that we gather from this hurricane and shipwreck is the safety of the Christian.
Some by swimming, "some on boards, and some on
broken pieces of the ship. And so it came to pass,
that they escaped all safe to land." They were all
saved because they were in God's keeping. Paul
was to be saved, and through him all that ship's
company—passengers, officers, crew, and prisoners.
Not one of them was lost. The hurricane could
smash and destroy their ship, but it could not hurt
them.

Life has its storms, its dangers, its trials, its sorrows, its shipwrecks; but those who put their trust
in God, those who believe in Christ and are true to
him, come through in triumph. He keeps his promise that he is able to keep them from falling and to
present them faultless before the presence of his
glory. See what happened to Paul that night. The
storm could not drown him. The cruel soldiers,
who planned to do so, could not kill him with their
swords; and when he was gathering sticks for the

fire about w...ich the refugees were warming themselves, and that viper fastened its fangs in his arm,
Paul suffered no harm, but shook it off into the
fire. On land or on sea, in the air, or under the
sea, or under the earth, the true Christian man is
always safe. His soul can suffer no harm. He can
come off conquerer and more than conqueror through
Him that loved us and gave himself for us.

I suppose they called the roll that night after all
the ship's company had gathered about the fire. I
can see one of the officers holding the parchment on
which the names of all the officers and seamen and
soldiers and prisoners were written. He holds it
near to the flame of the fire so that the centurion
can read the names that are inscribed on it. I hear
the centurion with his loud military voice calling the
roll: "Marcellus, merchant from Corinth?" "Present!" "Julius, Roman centurion?" "Present!"
"Aristarchus, Christian from Caesarea?" "Present!" "Maximus, master of the ship?" "Present!" "Olynthus, supercargo of the ship?"
"Present!" "Brutus, soldier of the legion?"
"Present!" "Luke, traveling physician from An-
tioch?" "Present!" "Paul, Hebrew prisoner on
his way to Rome?" "Present!" Two hundred and
seventy-six souls! All present, all safe on the land.
So, when the storms of life are past, and God's people land at length on the heavenly shore, and the

Captain of our Salvation calls the roll, not one will be missing. "And so it came to pass, that they escaped all safe to land."

There at length we shall gather, not by a bonfire kindled by the barbarians on bleak and rain-soaked Malta, but upon Canaan's happy shore; and there, by the sea of glass mingled with fire, and lighted by His love, we shall sing His power to save.

V

THE NIGHT OF REPENTANCE

"And Peter went out, and wept bitterly."
LUKE 22:62

MIDNIGHT ON THE MOUNT OF OLIVES. THE FULL
passover moon is shining in the Syrian sky, bath-
ing mountain, valley, hillside, and plain, and the
ancient city of David in its soft light. Below us is
the valley of Kedron, and on the other side rise the
huge walls of Jerusalem with their tremendous foundations and massive gates. Within the walls we
can see the Temple of Herod, its great door of
Corinthian brass—the Gate Beautiful—plainly vis-
ible in the moonlight. Silence reigns everywhere—
not a stir of life on this mountainside; not a light,
nor a sound of traffic, from the distant city.

But now the silence is broken. Walking down
the slope of Olivet and through the Garden of Gethsemane, where the ancient olive trees cast their
shadows over the ground, suddenly we hear a voice
of anguish. It is the sound of sobbing. It is the
voice of a man crying. I have heard all kinds of
crying. I have heard the cry of a little child that
was lost. I have heard the cry of the young woman
betrayed and abandoned by a faithless lover. I have

[70]

heard the cry of a mother over the grave of her child. I have heard the cry of the woman who had been overcome by temptation. But the cry that has always moved me most is the cry of a strong man. That is what we hear tonight at the midnight hour in the shadows of Gethsemane.

The man who is crying so strongly and so bitterly is Peter. We shall not invade the territory of his grief. He has come hither from the palace of Caiaphas, where, only an hour ago, he cursed and denied his Lord. This is the meaning of these terrible tears and this voice of agony that echoes through Gethsemane. What was it, Peter, that brought you to this place? Were there not other nearer, and equally secluded, places where you could have gone and knelt alone in your agony? But you have come here to Gethsemane. Was it because you felt that the only place where you could express your grief was where your Lord entered into his agony? Was it because you felt that the only fitting place for you to shed your tears was where your Lord shed his tears of blood while you slept, unhearing and unheeding? Yet in the echo of your sobs and cries we hear the note of hope and restoration. Yours, Peter, is the godly sorrow that worketh repentance. In some other secluded place, perhaps not far from this very spot where you are kneeling, Peter, another of your band of Twelve goes apart and kneels in the agony of his remorse. But in his cry and in his sobs, the cries and sobs of Judas, who betrayed his Lord, I hear no voice of repentance, but only the echo of remorse and of doom.

But we are not here to judge Peter nor to condemn him. Rather we are to let Peter preach to us, that he may both warn us and encourage us, and tell us of the marvelous forgiving love of Christ.

PETER'S TEMPTATION AND FALL

At the Supper, when Christ had said that the disciples who were gathered about him that night would forsake him and desert him in his hour of need and trial, Peter was strong and urgent in his protest and in his avowal of loyalty even unto death. "Lord, I am ready," he said, "to go with thee, both into prison, and to death." We miss it altogether here, if we say that Peter was just a rash, impetuous, impulsive man, boasting that his loyalty would stand firm when that of the other disciples had failed. That is altogether wrong. If any man ever meant what he said, Peter meant what he said that night when he declared that he would be faithful even unto death and that he was ready to go with Christ to prison and death. If at that moment, sitting there by the side of Christ, the Roman authorities had given Peter the alternative of prison and death, or renouncing and denying Christ, I have not the slightest doubt as to which Peter would have chosen. I am sure he would have permitted himself to be led away to prison and death by the side of Christ and for the sake of Christ. When he said, "I am ready to go with thee, both into prison, and to death," he was just as sincere—and probably more so—as you are when you sing, "O Jesus, I have promised to serve thee to the end." But that was Peter at his best moment; that was Peter in the close and loving fellowship of Christ, not "afar off" from him. Do you, too, not have your best and higher moment when, in all sincerity, you can pledge yourself to the noblest actions and to the highest loyalty to Christ? But do you not also remember other moments when it was a different self who spoke, and a different man who acted? Let him who does not know the difference in his own life between some high and noble and uplifting moment and mood of life, and another moment and mood of ignominy and shame, cast the first stone at Peter.

Peter had been well warned that night. One would have thought that the special warning would have kept him awake there in the Garden of Gethsemane, when Jesus entered into his agony, even though James and John slept at his side. And, in a way, Christ must have thought so too; for when he came and found them sleeping and awakened the three, it was not to John and not to James that he spoke, but to Peter, "Simon, ... couldest not thou watch one hour? . . . . The spirit truly is ready, but the flesh is weak." Remember that! No matter how strong our religious emotions, how clear our religious purpose, the flesh, this fallen nature within us, is always weak. Or, we might put it the other way: it is always strong, and ready to attack every good resolution and every devotion to righteousness and to Christ on our part.

When the mob came and began to manhandle Jesus, Peter drew the sword that he had brought with him and struck a great blow at one whom he saw maltreating his Lord. When you see him strike that blow you feel like crying, "Well done, Peter; you are living up to your promise." Certainly there was no sign there of cowardice or of weakness. And yet Peter is on the path to a terrible disaster and a shameful fall. Let us look at some of the preparatory steps in that terrible decline and fall.

One element in Peter's fall, one certain preparation for it, was that that night he followed his Master "afar off." We gather from the records that after the arrest of Christ all the disciples left Jesus and fled, just as he had said they would do. But two of them, Peter and John, evidently thought better of it. Recovering from their fright, they turned back to see what would become of Jesus. When the procession reached the palace of the high priest,

John, a little bolder than Peter, was evidently marching abreast with it, for he went in with the others, the officers and the crowd that had gathered. But Peter came up afterwards, and had to be admitted by the plea of John.

He followed his Lord afar off. Yonder is the procession proceeding down the slopes of Gethsemane, across the bridge over the Kedron, up the winding road, and through the gate into the city. You can see their torches dancing in the night, and the south wind brings to your ears the hoarse murmur of the voice of the mob. And there is Peter following, but afar off; now secreting himself behind a great olive tree, now crouching down behind a wall. He is determined to see where they take Jesus and what becomes of him, yet he is fearful for his own safety—and, in a way, he has good reason to be, for he was the only one of the disciples who had dared to assault one of the bodyguards of the high priest.

He did not openly desert or forsake Christ, but he followed him afar off; and by so doing Peter was marching into danger and into temptation. Unless you yourself have never followed your Lord "afar off," do not ever cast a stone at Peter, or hold him up to judgment and to ridicule. Have you yourself never skulked, as it were, behind the wall, or hid beyond the olive tree, when your Lord was in the hands of his enemies and needed a friend at his side? When an army is on the march in a hostile country, it is easy for armed bands to cut off stragglers. A straggler is an easy victim for Satan. How near are you to your Lord, those of you who have confessed his name and have promised to be faithful even unto death, as Peter promised? How wide is the gap between you and your Lord? When you give up the reading of the Bible, when you give up prayer, when you give up regular church attendance, you are following your Lord "afar off," and Satan has his eye upon you.

Another step towards Peter's fall was that he disguised his discipleship. We gather from the account in the Gospels that John went forward into the chamber where Jesus was on trial before Caiaphas; but Peter, pretending that he was just one of the crowd hostile to Jesus, sat down about the fire in the courtyard with the servants and soldiers and officers. This was the real beginning of Peter's denial. Long before he denied with his lips that he was a follower of Jesus, he had *acted* a denial of Christ. He did that when he sat down among the enemies of Christ just as if he belonged to their crowd. There he is, sitting with the rest of them, yet keeping well out of the glare of the fire, lest someone should recognize him.

There are times when men who are not true

friends of Christ join the company of those who are and try to act and speak as if they too are true friends of Christ. They tone down their worldly accent. But here we have the very opposite. Here is a man who tries to act as if he were an enemy of Christ. He tries hard, but in vain, to make his provincial Galilean accent sound just like that of the Judeans among whom he is sitting. That is always hard to do. Whether a man is a hypocrite in that he pretends to be a friend of Christ when he is not, or a hypocrite like Peter was that night, pretending to be an enemy of Christ when he was at heart a friend, it is always hard, yea, impossible, finally, to do it successfully; for, as in the case of Peter on this night, there is always something that betrays the real man. "Thy speech bewrayeth thee."

Peter was a friend of Christ, but he did not want anyone to know it. Is that so strange, after all? When Christ, or his Church, or his cause, was being assailed, have you never sat in silence, just as if the sentiments expressed were your own, just as if you too were an enemy of Christ? Let him who has never done that cast the first stone at Peter!

The next step after disguising our discipleship, as we so often do in close fellowship with the world, warming ourselves at the fire of the world's comfort and pleasure and society, is open denial. Suddenly, unexpectedly, the challenge comes, "Art thou not also one of his disciples?" And then, too often, comes the terrible, tragic, and sad answer, "I know not the man."

The stage is now set for Peter's fall. All the elements of disaster are there. He had followed him afar off. He had come without any living hope or faith, but only "to see the end." Then he sat down among the enemies of Christ, trying to act just as if he were an enemy. The next thing that happens is that he is compelled either to confess that he is just acting a part and that he is a friend and disciple of Christ, or that he is now his enemy.

Even in Peter's denial of Christ there was a progression of iniquity and sin. The first challenge and accusation seems to have been made by one of the maidservants of the high priest. John says that she was the one that let Peter in. When she saw his face she said, "Art not thou also one of this man's disciples?" According to Mark, Peter did not openly deny it, but did so by equivocation, for he said, "I know not, neither understand I what thou sayest." It was as if he had said, "You say I belong to Jesus of Nazareth? Girl, I don't know what you are talking about." That too is a very common form of denial of Christ. A man will not openly say that he renounces Christ and that he is against him, but he will not openly confess him.

His silence will permit the inference to be drawn that he is no friend of Christ's.

Peter did not feel happy, of course, after he said that he did not understand what the maid was talking about or what she wanted of him. Indeed, he felt so wretched and miserable—and, no doubt, so alarmed—that he got up from the circle about the fire, where he had been sitting, and went out into the porch, near the entrance to the palace. He had no sooner got there than the cock crew. Perhaps that made him think of the words of Christ, how the cock would not crow twice before he had thrice denied him. But probably not. Probably Peter did not think then of the words of Jesus. After a little, restless and uneasy, he went back and joined the group around the fire. He had no sooner sat down than either the same maid or another, looking at him closely by the light of the fire, turned and said to the men and the officers who sat around, "This man was also with him." This time Peter openly denied Christ, and said, "I know him not. [I am not his disciple.]"

Another hour passed; and you can imagine Peter's feelings during that time. He had commenced by denial and lying, and now it seemed to Peter that there was no other course for him but to brazen and lie it out. Yet his soul was in agony within him, you can be sure of that.

O, what a tangled web we weave,
When first we practise to deceive! [1]

Here you have the sequence of sin. One sin opens
the gate for another. One sin introduces another.
The first sin demands the second, and the second
demands the third. After an hour had passed, this
is what happened: Peter's chief dread, of course,
was that he should be recognized by the man he had
wounded with the sword in the Garden of Gethsemane, or by one of his friends. Now his dread
was realized. A servant of the high priest, a relative of the man whose ear Peter had cut off, came up
to the fire to warm himself. As he looked around,
his eye suddenly fell upon Peter. Shaking him by
the shoulder, he said, "Did not I see thee in the
garden with him?" This time, thoroughly enraged
and frightened, Peter leaped to his feet and began to
curse and to swear, "I know not the man."

Terrible was the fall of Peter. And yet Peter
was no monster, no prodigy of iniquity. Oh, those
words of the relative of the man Peter had wounded
in the Garden of Gethsemane—"Did I not see thee
in the garden with him?" As if to say, "Does not
the fact that you were there in the garden with
him confess that you are his friend, in spite of the
fact that you sit about the fire with his enemies and

[1] From "Marmion," by Sir Walter Scott.

declare with your loud fisherman's oaths that you never knew him?" Oh, those words, "Did not I see thee in the garden with him"! Will no one ever take you and me by the shoulder and look into our faces and say, "Did not I see thee in the garden with him? Did not I see thee in the church with him? Did not I see thee singing the hymns? Did not I see thee teaching the Sunday-school class? Did not I see thee drinking the sacramental wine of his Blood? And now, where is this that I find you, and what are these words that I hear you say?"

THE REPENTANCE OF PETER

Great as was the fall of Peter, still greater was his repentance. In that divine repentance there were two factors. One was just an incident of the natural world, the crowing of the cock. Christ had chosen that common thing of animal life as the sign of the fall of Peter, and also as one of the means of his restoration. How many times before had Peter heard a cock crow! But now it was different. The voice of God, the voice of conscience, was speaking in that crowing of the cock, and saying to Peter, "Thou art the man! Oh, Peter, you have sinned. Peter, before it is too late, repent and return unto your God." When Peter heard the cock crow the second time, he remembered the words of Jesus foretelling his denial, and when he thought thereon he wept.

Just the crowing of the cock! Yes, God can use events like that to speak to our soul, to make us remember, to make us weep the tears of repentance. Blessed be anything, whether it be the crowing of the cock or the voice of a preacher, a book or a sermon, a face or a place, a hymnbook, an old portrait, a bit of lace, a worn Bible, an old letter—blessed, I say, be anything that makes you think about your soul, about your better moments, about your nobler purpose, about your higher and divine self! Perhaps this night someone shall hear the crowing of that cock.

The second factor in Peter's repentance and restoration was that look of Jesus. After all, it was that, timed to the crowing of the cock, that was the decisive thing—the thing that broke Peter's heart and worked repentance in his soul. When Jesus looked, just as he heard Peter's loud oaths of denial, it was then that Peter remembered the words of the Lord; and when he thought thereon he went out and wept bitterly.

Sometimes I think I would like to ask the angels and the archangels to describe for me, if even they are able to do it, that look on the Saviour's face when he turned and looked upon Peter. For in that look was all the length and the breadth, and the depth and the height of the love of God which passeth understanding. All revelation and all redemption, and all heaven too, are concentrated there. But even without the help of the angels and the archangels, I know that in that look which Christ gave Peter there was that that brought Peter to himself and also revealed to him the pity and the love of God.

Peter did not look on Christ. He would have been glad to look in any other direction than that. No; it was Jesus who turned and looked upon Peter. That is where true repentance begins. It begins with God. It is God's greatest gift. Did Jesus not look upon Judas, too? I am sure that he did. I know that he looked upon him when he washed his feet that night at the Supper. I know that he looked upon him in the Garden of Gethsemane when he said to him, "Betrayest thou the Son of man with a kiss?" It was the same face. It was the same love that shone in it. But how different the fate of those two men! Judas rejected that look of Christ and was lost. Peter responded to it and repented and was saved. How marvelous was that look!

Christ called and convicted and saved Peter with a look. He did not speak a word. There was no loud cry of pain or amazement or anger. There was no gesture of the hand. There was not even a softest, gentlest whisper of his voice; but only that look. What was in that look? There was in it that which revealed Peter to himself and made him loathe himself. And yet there was in it, too, that infinite pity and sorrow and love and desire which made Peter hope, and made him repent and come back to God. That look must have said to Peter: "I go to die upon the cross, Peter. You have denied me thrice, but Satan has not yet gained possession of thee. Repent now, Peter, even now, and it will not be too late. Remember my prayer for thee. Hold fast to me, and thy faith will not fail thee."

I would like to have seen Peter's face that night, when he went out after Jesus looked upon him and wept bitterly; for, although his face must have shown deep distress, I am sure that it revealed the highest beauty that can come to the face of man—the beauty of repentance.

It is repentance that gives to the soul its highest beauty; and the angels themselves, Christ said, rejoice when they see the look of repentance on the face of man. Today that same Saviour looks out over the world with the same look of love that was in his face when he looked upon the face of Peter. Who will answer that look and repent, and repent now? That, undoubtedly, was the last look that Peter had from Jesus before he died upon the Cross. Again Christ looks, and for some of you it may be the *last* look. Will you answer that look, as cursing, swearing, denying Peter answered it of old, that night in the courtyard there at Jerusalem?

VI

THE NIGHT THAT KNEW NO MORNING

"And it was night."

JOHN 13:30

IN MY DREAM I WAS CARRIED AWAY TO A GREAT and high mountain where I saw that great city, the goal of all our hopes and desires, the end of our Salvation, the Holy City of God, the New Jerusalem. Around the city, as around the earthly Jerusalem, there ran a wall great and high. There were twelve gates, north, south, east, and west; and every gate was a pearl, and at every gate stood one of the Great Angels. On the gates were written the names of the Twelve Tribes of the Children of Israel, from Reuben to Benjamin. The wall of the city stood upon twelve massive foundation stones, and on each stone was the name of one of the Twelve Apostles of the Lamb; and as I walked around the city, thrilling with joy and rapture at the glory and splendor of it, I read the names written upon the twelve stones—Peter, James, John, and all the others. But one name was missing. I looked in vain for that name, either on the twelve gates or on the twelve foundation stones—and that name was Judas.

[85]

The longest night in the history of the world is drawing to a close. The night is passing, but the day has not yet come. Far to the east, over the mountains of Moab, there is just the faintest intimation of the coming day. The huge walls of Jerusalem and the towers and pinnacles of the Temple are emerging from the shadows of the night. In the half darkness and half light I can make out a solitary figure coming down the winding road from the wall of Jerusalem towards the gorge of the Kedron. On the bridge over the brook he pauses for a moment and, turning, looks back towards the Holy City. Then he goes forward for a few paces and, again turning, halts and looks up towards the massive walls of the city. Again he turns, and this time he does not stop. Now I can see that in his hand he carries a rope. Up the slope of Olivet he comes and, entering in at the gate of Gethsemane, walks under the trees of the Garden. Seizing with his arms one of the low-branching limbs of a gnarled olive tree, he draws himself up into the tree. Perhaps he is the proprietor of this part of the Garden, and has come to gather the olives. But why with a rope? For a little he is lost to my view in the springtime foliage of the tree. Then, suddenly, I see his body plummet down like a rock from the top of the tree. Yet the body does not reach the ground, but is suspended in mid-air. And there it swings slowly to and fro, at the end of a rope.

"And [Judas] went out and hanged himself." This, then, Judas, is thine end; and here to this Garden of Gethsemane, where thy Master in his agony shed his tears of blood, and where thou didst implant upon his lips thy traitorous kiss, and where for the last time he called thee friend, here to Gethsemane thou hast come to end thy life, and, if possible, expiate thy great crime and sin. As thy fellow disciples said of thee, Judas, thou wentest to thine "own place," the place of thine own choosing and thine own desire, not the place that thou mightest have had, not the place that thy Master desired for thee. And to that dreadful place thou wentest in spite of the warnings and in spite of the appeals of thy Master.

Judas "went immediately out: and it was night." That is the way in which John brings to a conclusion his account of the tremendous drama of that last night, when, just before the institution of the Lord's Supper, Judas, having received from the hand of Christ the sop, as a token that he was the one who would betray him, "went immediately out: and it was night." This was the night that knew no morning, the night when a soul rejected the last overtures of Divine Mercy and chose his own place of darkness and of doom. Always that phrase of

John's, "and it was night," will stand for the darkness and loneliness and separation of sin. It will stand for the gloom and sorrow which settle down upon the soul which knowingly and finally rejects the Lord Jesus Christ. There were other dark nights that came down over men in the Bible—the darkness that came down over Pharaoh, the darkness of Saul's night when he resorted to a witch, the darkness of Peter's night when he went out and wept bitterly— but here is the darkest night of all, the night that never knew a morning. Here we have the separation that is wrought by sin.

SIN SEPARATES A MAN FROM HIS FRIENDS

I sometimes wonder if, when he went out that night from the upper chamber, Judas lingered for a little on the path, looking back perhaps at the light in the room where Jesus was with the eleven disciples. Even then did he think that he might turn and go back? But whether he did or not, how lonely he was! His was the part now to follow the movements of Christ and his disciples that night, and see where he went when the Supper was over, so that he could notify his enemies, the priests and the Pharisees. "[He] was guide," the evangelist writes, "to them that took Jesus." What a guide! Yet we are all guides—guides to light or guides to darkness. So there is Judas, hiding behind a wall, or the ledge of a rock, as Jesus and his companions come down the path to cross the Kedron, singing as they go, on their way to Gethsemane. That was his company. These were the friends of Judas; that was where he belonged; but now, for him the night of separation and loneliness.

Sin always separates. Cain went out from the presence of the Lord when he had sinned. Gehazi sinned and went out from Elisha, a leper white as snow. Jacob sinned and went out into the wilderness at Bethel a frightened fugitive. Peter sinned and went out from the high priest's court to weep bitterly. Always out, always away from friends, always into loneliness and darkness.

One hour before his fatal duel with Alexander Hamilton, Aaron Burr, sitting in his library at Richmond Hill in New York, wrote to his beloved daughter Theodosia: "Some very wise man has said, 'O fools, who think it solitude to be alone.' This is but poetry. Let us therefore drop the subject, lest it lead on to another on which I have imposed silence on myself." Even then, before the fatal shot was fired and the bloody deed was done, he felt the loneliness of sin. In a few hours he was a fugitive from the sudden and deep abhorrence of his fellow citizens, his political career over forever, and his great ambitions wrecked. Henceforth, like Cain, he was a fugitive and a vagabond on the face of the earth.

For the rest of his life, until he died in poverty and obscurity and utter loneliness in the very city where he had risen to so great renown, Aaron Burr was a man without a country—almost without a friend. It was the bitter truth he uttered when, informed of the death of his beautiful daughter Theodosia, he said, "I am severed from mankind." There are lonely people in our cities today, and thousands who carry heavy and difficult burdens of grief, anxiety, or pain, and disappointment. But the loneliest soul of all is the man whose transgression has raised up a wall, not of brick or mortar or stone, yet terribly real, between him and his fellow men. Yes, sin separates us from our friends.

SIN SEPARATES A MAN FROM HIS TRUE AND BEST SELF

Many a man is living with his false and worse self, and is alienated from his true self. The prodigal went out from his father's house and followed his false self into a far country—to the house of harlots and gamblers and sinners, until at length he came clear down to the swine. Then he discovered his true self, for "he came to himself" and said, "I will arise and go to my father." Nothing is sadder than when a man finds that his transgressions and follies, his inner disloyalties, have disqualified him for service to the highest and to the best.

THE NIGHT THAT KNEW NO MORNING

In Tennyson's story "The Holy Grail," the knight,
Sir Percivale, set out to seek it with enthusiasm.
Lifted up in heart and thought because of his late
prowess in the lists, and confident that he has the
strength for the great enterprise, he goes forth on
the holy quest. The heavens never appeared so
blue, nor the earth so green, and all his blood dances
within him. Then, suddenly, there comes back to
him the warning of King Arthur, that most of those
who sought the Grail would follow wandering fires
and fail in their quest. Then the knight remembers
his sins and feels himself unworthy of the holy task:

Then every evil word I had spoken once,
And every evil thought I had thought of old,
And every evil deed I ever did,
Awoke and cried, "This Quest is not for thee."
And lifting up mine eyes, I found myself
Alone, and in a land of sand and thorns,
And I was thirsty even unto death;
And I, too, cried, "This Quest is not for thee."

What could be sadder than to hear the trumpet
call of a great and holy cause, and watch others go
forth to the battle, but ourselves have to hang back
because we feel unfitted for the holy enterprise?
Therefore, let us be "loyal to the royal that is within
us." Let us so live today that tomorrow our mouth
shall not be covered, nor our uplifted arm, ready

to strike for truth, paralyzed by the memory of past transgressions.

SIN SEPARATES FROM PEACE OF MIND

In Byron's great drama *Cain,* when Cain and his wife and child are about to leave their home and go out into the land of Nod, away from the presence of the Lord, Adah, Cain's wife, turning to look at the body of the fallen Abel, says, "Peace be with him!" But Cain answers, "But with *me!*" And there the great drama comes to a close. The suggestion of that exclamation of Cain, "But with *me!*" is more powerful than any stanza or paragraph to tell that with Cain there was no peace.

"But with *me!*" The drama of sin always ends there. It leaves man separated from his peace. Fears may die, but not remorse. John Randolph, when he was dying in Philadelphia, kept repeating the word, "Remorse! Remorse!" He demanded that a dictionary be brought so that he could study its meaning. When no dictionary could be found, he had the physician write it out for him on a piece of paper—"Remorse." If hell were just the invention of pale-faced theologians, long ago the race would have cast the idea overboard. But it still remains, because it is not the invention of men who write books or uphold systems of thought; it is the deep affirmation of the human heart. Remorse is like the ground swell in the ocean after a storm. The storm has subsided; the sky is blue; the air is balmy; there is not a whitecap to be seen; but the ship heaves and tosses because of the mighty swell that remains. So remorse heaves the soul as the tide heaves the ocean. To sin is to say farewell to peace. Come up hither and preach, ye who have come to my study; ye whose tears I have seen, whose sobs I have heard, whose chains I have vainly sought to unloose, come hither, I say, and tell me if the way of sin is not farewell to peace.

SIN SEPARATES A MAN FROM GOD

All that we have said thus far about the separating power of sin is summed up in this: Sin separates us from God. That is what the prophet said long ago. "Your iniquities have separated between you and your God, and your sins have hid his face from you." That was what Cain dreaded when he went out from the presence of the Lord, and said in his lamentation, "And from thy face shall I be hid." That was what David feared would be his final state after his infamous transgression of adultery and murder, when he prayed, "Cast me not away from thy presence; and take not thy holy spirit from me." That was the first thing that sin did. It hid man from God, when the man and the woman hid themselves amid the trees of the Garden when they heard

[93]

the voice of the Lord God. And that is the last thing that sin will do, when in the Last Great Day guilty sinners shall call upon the rocks to fall upon them and the mountains to hide them from the face of Him that sitteth upon the throne.

But we have all sinned. Not only Cain and David and Judas, but all have sinned, and our sins have separated us from God. We could never go back to that lost fellowship, if it were left to us. But God in his mercy takes means to secure that his banished be not exiled forever from him. This same Christ who was betrayed by Judas, denied by Peter, crowned with thorns, and crucified between two thieves, has built a bridge of reconciliation by which we can come back to God. "God was in Christ, reconciling the world unto himself." To them that are afar off he hath made peace through the Blood of his Cross.

How strange a shadow on this last night is Judas. In one way, he is an enigma: first, that a man who dipped his hand with Jesus in the dish could then go out and betray him; but more because of this, that his part is declared ready and prepared for him, and that what he did was in fulfillment of a divine plan, "that the scriptures . . . . might be fulfilled." Yet one asks, "If Judas played his appointed part in this tragedy of Redemption, how can he be blamed?" But there is no doubt that he was blamed and condemned. The apostles condemned him; Christ condemned him and called him the son of perdition; and Judas condemned himself when he brought back the blood money and then went out and hanged himself. All that we can say, when we face this mystery in the life of Judas—or in the life of another—is that although he plays an appointed part, and God knows the end from the beginning, Judas was the author and the architect of his own transgression and his own doom.

The apostles who had been associated with Judas were careful to refrain from angry comments on his traitorous deed. When the apostles and the disciples were about to select a successor to Judas, all that they said was that Judas fell away and went "to his own place."

Not a word of censure, or blame, or amazement, but merely that Judas went "to his own place." Yes, it was his own place. He went out into the night. But no one drove him out. Christ did not order him to go; the other disciples did not drive him from their fellowship. Judas went out of his own free will and accord. He went to his own place. It was a place of gloom, of guilt, of remorse, of loneliness, and of final despair; but it was *his* place; it was the house that he had built. He laid the foundations; he raised the beams; he built the rooms; he decorated its walls. Judas went to his own place.

That is true of all of us. We think we are greatly influenced and moved, happily or unhappily, by those with whom we live or with whom we work in life; but, in the last analysis, we go to our own place and build our own life. That is true of the life to come. We need no terrifying symbols or figures of speech to describe the punishments of the future. It is not so much that God condemns and punishes a man, as that a man condemns and punishes himself. He goes to his own place. Let it stand at that.

> The tissues of the life to be
>   We weave with colors all our own;
> And on the fields of destiny,
>   We reap as we have sown.

When Christ gave the sop to Judas, that was for him the truce of God. Then, even at the last, he might have turned. That was his chance, his moment of opportunity and of grace. But he let it pass, and went out. "And it was night."

Christ would have none of us go out into the night. "He that followeth me," he said, "shall not walk in darkness." In different ways Christ makes his final appeal, and offers to the soul the truce of God. It may be in the judgments, the punishments, which have fallen upon you in some wrong course, and, like a flash at midnight, have shown you the danger and the path to safety. It may be in some sorrow or affliction that has softened your heart. It may be in some disappointment or overthrow of earthly expectation. It may be in some gracious token of his longsuffering and his patience. So God speaks to the soul and calls it back from the darkness into the light. Peter, like Judas, went out into the night. But the grace that Christ offered him when he looked upon him in the priest's court-yard, as his wild denying oaths were ringing out, that grace Peter received; and in the night he wept his way back to repentance and to faith. Judas also went out, and it was night—but a night without a morning. Which shall it be? May God help us all to choose light and not darkness.

VII

THE NIGHT WITH THE MEDIUM

"And they came to the woman by night."
I Samuel 28:8

By night! And, as we shall see, from him who came, it was night in two ways—night in that the day was over and the sun was gone, but night also in that darkness had come down over the soul. John said of Judas that when he went out "it was night." Perhaps John meant only the time of the day; but reading his narrative we know that for Judas it was a night that knew no morning. So it was for this great man of the Old Testament who came to the woman by night.

Gilboa's mountain is wrapped in gloom. Far off in the distant valley there is the occasional flash of a torch, and now and then on the evening wind comes the faint echo of a trumpet in the camp of the army of the Philistines. Here on this side of the mountain is a cavern, and by the mouth of the cave sits a venerable witch, a woman with a "familiar spirit," who has, or claims to have, power over the unseen world.

Suddenly, as the woman sits by her steaming caldron, there appears at the mouth of the cave a man of great stature, accompanied by two other men, all of them in complete disguise. The cautious witch reminds her visitors of the royal commandment against the trade of the soothsayer and the death penalty upon those who invoke the dead. But the tall stranger guarantees her protection and safety. "As the Lord liveth," he says to her, "there shall no punishment happen to thee for this thing." Then the woman asks, "Whom shall I bring up unto thee?" Her visitor, who is the disguised king of Israel, Saul, answers, "Bring me up Samuel."

The witch went through her ritual and incantations, and then to her amazement and terror Samuel himself appeared, and the woman knew that her client was none other than King Saul. The king, who apparently at first either did not see Samuel or did not recognize him, quieting her fears, said to the woman, "What sawest thou?" She answered, I saw gods ascending out of the earth." Saul said to her, "What form is he of?" The woman answered, "An old man cometh up; and he is covered with a mantle." By this time Saul knew that he was in the presence of Samuel, and bowed down in his presence—one of the few times, perhaps the only time in his life, when Saul bowed down. O Saul, if thou hadst only bowed down to Samuel, and bowed down to God earlier in thy life, this terrible last chapter in thy life might never have been written.

Samuel and Saul had often met in the past, since that first meeting when, seeking his father's lost asses, Saul came to Samuel's house, and Samuel, knowing that he was the chosen of the Lord, anointed him with oil and kissed him. But it was now a long time since Saul and Samuel had parted. Not since the day after which it is written that "Samuel came no more to see Saul until the day of his death" had they met. This final interview must have been a painful one for Samuel. It must have been hard for him to pronounce the doom and death of King Saul, for Samuel had loved Saul and more than once had prayed for him and wept over him. But now Saul's day of grace is over.

To the prostrate king, Samuel said sternly, "Why hast thou disquieted me, to bring me up?" Saul answered that he had come to him out of his great distress, that a battle was to be fought with the Philistines on the morrow, and that God had departed from him, and he could get no answer, either by prophets, or by dreams. Hence he had come to Samuel, hoping that he would advise him and tell him what he should do. To this Samuel replied, "Wherefore then dost thou ask of me, seeing the Lord is departed from thee, and is become thine enemy?" Then Samuel, reminding Saul of his past transgressions and his rebellion against God, told him that the end was at hand and that he would die in the battle of the morrow. "Tomorrow shalt thou and thy sons be with me."

In the great battle which was fought the next day on the slopes of Mount Gilboa, Israel was defeated and Saul's army fled; but Saul fought on with his old-time courage and heroism, until he was dangerously wounded by the Philistine archers. When his three sons had fallen dead at his side, then Saul, seeing that he had lost his kingdom and had lost his sons, and had nothing further to live for, took a sword and fell on it. He had reached the *ultima Thule,* the beyond which nothing, of human woe and misery.

THE INFLUENCE OF GOOD MEN

There was never a day or a night in all the Bible which so declares the influence of a good man, the abiding power of a righteous personality. How moving was that request of Saul that the witch of Endor should call up Samuel. "Whom shall I bring up?" she said to the king. And for whom did Saul ask? Not for Moses, the great leader of the people; not for Joshua, the famous captain of the host; not for Gideon, who in that very valley had put the Midianites to flight. No, none of those great heroes of the past; but one Saul knew far better, "Bring me up Samuel! Samuel, who anointed me king and kissed me at the spring of the day; Samuel, who warned me; Samuel, who wept over me. Bring me up Samuel! If any man can help me or deliver me now, or tell me my fate, that man is Samuel. Bring me up Samuel!"

"Bring me up Samuel!" Sublime tribute that, on the part of God-rejecting Saul to Samuel. That is the way to live, to pass through the world so that somewhere someone in some trial or crisis of life will think of you and wish to call you up. Have you never done that yourself in some dark night of sorrow, or trial, or perplexity, or when the cup of agony was at your lip? Have you not called up some godly father, or mother, or other friend of God, who was also your friend, and, looking into his face, and remembering his words, found strength sufficient for your trial? Yes; thank God, there are those whom we can call up.

A WASTED LIFE

That was the tragedy about Saul that struck David so sadly when in his sublime ode over the death of Saul and Jonathan he said that "the shield of the mighty is vilely cast away, the shield of Saul, as though he had not been anointed with oil." So great a tragedy was it that David apostrophized the very mountains of Gilboa, and demanded of them that there be neither dew nor rain upon their sides, for there it was that Saul fell, disowned and dishonored.

Saul is one of the first three or four men of the Bible that I would like to see in heaven. For some reason, after Paul and David, I would like to talk with Saul as well as with any man in the Bible. I wonder sometimes if we shall have that opportunity. Browning's "Saul" is a great, but somewhat obscure, poem. Yet he says one thing about Saul that is easily understood:

> . . . . The same, God did choose,
> To receive what a man may waste, desecrate, never quite lose.

Those last words, "Never quite lose," would seem to hold out a ray of hope for Saul's ultimate salvation. But that mystery we leave with God, who knoweth them that are his. The other two lines of the poem are not to be questioned—namely, that God did choose Saul to receive what a man may waste and desecrate. Saul's life illustrates the truth that great gifts can be wasted, that new hearts can be hardened and corrupted, and that only "he that endureth to the end shall be saved." How bright and promising was the morning of Saul's life, "the spring of the day," as the chronicler so beautifully puts it. Saul started out with notable graces and virtues, a man of humility, a man of courage, a man of magnanimity, a man of great opportunity; and yet this is the sad end of it all—Saul took a sword and fell on it. You who have been anointed, as it were, with oil, dedicated to God by your parents in the waters of baptism, consecrated by your own prayers and by the prayers of others too, what about your shield? Is it going to be vilely cast away, as though it had not been anointed with oil?

THE DESTROYING POWER OF JEALOUSY

After Samuel finally departed from Saul the last terrible chapter of Saul's life opens up before us. There is nothing like it, I think, in all human biography, in all history. Saul is like a man struggling in a vortex. He is like one of those heroes of Greek tragedy, battling with fate. He burns out like a volcano. Or, to change the figure, like a ship broken with the waves and blasted with the winds and scorched with the lightning, he drives through the sea, until at last, in awful darkness, he crashes on the rocks and is broken to pieces. What a chaos! What a tragedy and doom are Saul's jealousy, suspicion, insane anger, cruelty, murder, sacrilege, awful solitude, and remorse! And yet, with it all, pathetic appeals to David to heal him and deliver him from the evil spirit in his heart; turning to weep over David after he had tried to kill him; lifted once more into pathetic ecstasy when about to commit a murder; consulting a witch and a woman with a familiar spirit, and yet through her asking for the presence and counsel and prayers of the godliest man of the Bible.

The sacred writer explains this tumult and chaos in Saul's life, as far as it can be explained, by saying that "an evil spirit . . . . troubled him." One manifestation of that evil spirit is plain enough. It was the spirit of jealousy. Saul could never forget that Samuel had said to him that God was going to give the kingdom to another, a man "better than thou." He could never forget, either, that fatal song of the women after David's victory over the Philistine champion, "Saul hath slain his thousands, and David his ten thousands." From that day forward, Saul "eyed David." He loved him, and yet he hated him. He wept over him, yet sought to kill him. Nowhere else do we see so clearly the devastating power of jealousy. We wonder if Shakespeare, that great observer of the human heart, when he wrote that jealousy "is the green-eyed monster which doth mock the meat it feeds upon," had in mind King Saul, for never was there a life in which jealousy did so mock its victim as in the life of Saul.

Hawthorne was a man well qualified to take hold of this great study in psychology—the character of King Saul. We regret that he never did so. But in his tale of "The Bosom Serpent" he illustrates the power of jealousy to destroy a soul. The man who had been separated from his wife because of jealous suspicions would sometimes hold his hand to his bosom and exclaim, "It gnaws! It gnaws!" For this reason he was known to the people in the town as the man with the snake in his breast. Sometimes he would create great consternation and alarm when he stopped other men on the street and asked them how their serpent was. At length, after all kinds of remedies had been tried, his wife appeared and pleaded with him to forget himself and show his love for her. At that the man fell on the ground, and there was the sound like the passing of a serpent through the grass, and a tinkle was heard as if it had dropped into the fountain. Thus the man was cured of the bosom serpent of jealousy. What about the serpent in thy breast? Oh, beware of that bosom serpent of jealousy!

RESISTING THE HOLY SPIRIT

In a certain sense the ministry of Samuel to Saul was the ministry of the Holy Spirit to the soul of man. Time and time again Saul resisted and rejected the Holy Spirit as he spoke to him through Samuel, until at length we come to that fateful sentence, "And Samuel came no more to see Saul until the day of his death." Now when Saul called upon God in his distress, God answered him not. Can a man go so far away from God that he gets to a place where God does not answer? We judge from the life of Saul that that is so. God himself has said that his Spirit will not always strive with man. There comes a day when they will "call upon me, but I will not answer." The day of grace that is granted unto you and me, just as it was granted unto Saul, can be sinned away.

> There is a time, we know not when,
>   A point we know not where,
> That marks the destiny of men
>   To glory or despair.
>
> There is a line by us unseen,
>   That crosses every path;
> The hidden boundary between
>   God's patience and his wrath. . . . .
>
> How far may we go on in sin?
>   How long will God forbear?
> Where does hope end, and where begin
>   The confines of despair?
>
> An answer from the skies is sent;
>   "Ye that from God depart,
> While it is called today, repent,
>   And harden not your heart." [1]

[1] From "The Hidden Line," by J. Addison Alexander.

Saul made the mistake, sad and pathetic though it was, of thinking that Samuel could help him when God would not. Now hear what Samuel said. This is the only sermon preached to mortal men by one who came from the dead, and that alone would make it one of the most momentous sermons ever preached. Samuel said to Saul, "To morrow shalt thou and thy sons be with me." That was Samuel's last sermon to Saul, and the first, and only, sermon that was ever preached from the grave. And what was the meaning of that sermon, and of those words, "To morrow shalt thou and thy sons be with me"? It meant for Saul that his day of grace was over, that the time of repentance was past. And to you and me the words of Samuel preach that earnest, tender sermon, so often on the lips of the prophets and the apostles, and of Christ himself, the sermon that time is always preaching, "Now is the accepted time; behold, now is the day of salvation." Seek ye the Lord while he may be found, call ye upon him while he is near."

VIII

THE NIGHT ANGELS CLIMBED
A LADDER

"And he lighted upon a certain place, and
tarried there all night, because the sun was
set. . . . . And he dreamed, and behold a
ladder set up on the earth, and the top of it
reached to heaven: and behold the angels of
God ascending and descending on it."

GENESIS 28:11-12

A LONELY STRETCH ON THE SYRIAN DESERT. BARE
wastes of sand and tufts of grass amid the gaunt,
naked hills. Toward the west the sun has already
sunk below the horizon, and to the east the mountains are rapidly sinking into gloom as the dark
mantle of the oncoming night covers them.

Along the desert highway comes a solitary traveler. He is a young man in the vigor of life, but
when he comes nearer we can see in his face the
look of guilt and fear and dejection, as well as physical fatigue. Now and then he looks back over his
shoulder, as if to see if anyone is in pursuit of
him—and no wonder, for he has cheated his old
father and defrauded his brother out of the blessing,
and now has had to flee for his life. Sin always
drives a man out. It drove our first parents out of
the Garden of Eden. It drove this man out from his

father's house and his father's country. It drove Peter out into the night, where he wept bitterly; and Judas out into the night, where he hanged himself. Always out, always away from God!

The solitary traveler selects the side of a hill somewhat protected from the evening wind. He takes his wallet from off his shoulder and lays it with his staff on the ground. Then he places a stone for a pillow and, lying down, and covering his face with his mantle lest the moon should smite him by night, he sinks into the deep sleep of sorrow and exhaustion.

But as he sleeps he dreams. And what a dream it was, almost the loveliest thing in the Bible! And all the more wonderful because the dreamer was a man who so recently had committed so despicable a transgression. In his dream the young man saw a ladder set up on earth, the top of which reached to heaven, and the angels of God were ascending and descending upon it. At the top of the ladder stood the Lord, who told the youth that he was the God of his father and the God of his grandfather, and that the land upon which he was then lying and the whole country—north, south, east, and west—would belong to him and his descendants, and that in him and in his seed all families of the earth would be blessed. With this went the promise, too, that God would be with him in all places whither he went, and one day would bring him back in safety to his native land.

When the young man awoke after that beautiful dream, he exclaimed to himself, "Surely the Lord is in this place; and I knew it not. . . . . This is none other but the house of God, and this is the gate of heaven." So thrilled and impressed was he that he set up for a sacred pillar the very stone upon which his head had rested when he dreamed the dream, and poured oil upon it. Then, bowing down before it, he vowed a vow—the first recorded vow in all history—and said that if God would be with him and keep him in his way, and bring him again to his father's house in peace, he would follow the Lord as his God and make of this place where God had appeared to him an altar and come and worship. Then, taking up his staff and putting his wallet over his shoulder, the youth starts eastward again. Every now and then, as he goes, he turns to look for a moment back toward the place where he had dreamed the dream and had seen the ladder with the angels of God. Gradually his figure grows fainter and fainter, and dimmer and dimmer on the eastern horizon, and now it is lost all together.

A FADING DREAM

Down in Mesopotamia, in the employ of his mother's brother, Laban, this young man, who was

Jacob—in some respects the worst and the best man in the Bible—began the battle of life. In that struggle for success there was one beautiful episode, the romance of Jacob's life—his love for Rachel, for whom he served Laban seven years and said at the end that they seemed to him as so many days for the love he had for her. Jacob was more than a match for his hard, shrewd Shylock uncle Laban, and he prospered greatly, accumulating not only a family, but numerous flocks and herds. He had become a rich, powerful, and successful man. But there was one thing that Jacob had lost. He had lost the companionship of the angels. He was no longer a dreamer.

In the midst of his prosperity God spoke to him in Mesopotamia and told him to go back to his own country, reminding him that he was the God of Bethel, where he had vowed a vow unto God. Jacob then set out for his native land. On the way he was overcome with fear when he heard that his brother Esau was coming to meet him with four hundred men. While he waited in dread by the ford of the Jabbok, Jacob had his mysterious midnight wrestle with the angel, who blessed him, and called him Israel, the Prince of God. When he got back to his own country, instead of going at once to Bethel, as he had vowed he would do, he turned to the south and settled down in the lush pastures of

Shechem. There his sons and their families sank into idolatry, while Jacob's flocks and herds increased.

You would hardly recognize Jacob now as the man who had dreamed that dream and seen the angels at Bethel. If there were times when thoughts of Bethel came back to him and he remembered his vow that he would go there and worship, he quickly called for one of his sons, or one of his servants, to drive the sheep past his tent. Then he began to count: "One, ten, twenty, fifty, one hundred, two hundred, five hundred, a thousand, five thousand, ten thousand!" Then he called for the goats to be driven past him: "Five hundred, a thousand, five thousand!" And when they were gone, calling for the camels to be driven up, he counted them, while he rubbed his hands in delight.

Thus the years passed. If his conscience sometimes hurt him about those sons of his with their idols, he excused himself by saying, "Times are different now than when I was a boy in my father Isaac's house. Young people have different ideas today. They think for themselves now, and although I am sorry to see them worshiping idols, yet I can hardly forbid them." Thus the years went by, until thirty years had passed since God had appeared unto Jacob at Bethel and since Jacob had made his vow to return and worship there.

BACK TO HIS DREAM

Then God spake unto Jacob. How did God speak then to men? I suppose no differently than he speaks to men today. In what clearer, more impressive, more unmistakable way could God speak than through the voice of conscience? God cares as much for your soul as he did for the soul of Jacob, and he speaks to you just as clearly, just as earnestly, just as commandingly as he did to Jacob of old.

God said to Jacob, "Arise, go up to Bethel, and dwell there: and make there an altar unto God, that appeared unto thee when thou fleddest from the face of Esau thy brother." "Bethel!" Jacob said to himself. "Bethel, where I saw the angels! Bethel, where I heard the voice of God! Bethel, where I made the vow that I would return there and build an altar and there worship God!" Jacob knew that he was far from Bethel, not only in location, but in spirit. He thought of his indifference to the idolatry of his sons. He thought of the idols with which the tents were littered. How could he go to Bethel? And yet there was no doubt but that it was the voice of God that he had heard. In many respects Jacob was a man of strange inconsistencies; but give him credit for this—he did not try to take his idols with him to Bethel, to the house of God. He knew that idols and Bethel had nothing in common. The first thing he did was to collect all the idols from his sons and their families, and bury them beneath the oak trees. Then they set out on the journey to Bethel. You can imagine Jacob's thoughts and recollections as his mind ran back thirty years and he saw himself again the lonely frightened youth fleeing from the wrath of Esau.

It was not hard for him to find the very spot where he had slept that night. There are some places that you never forget. The stone on which his head had rested for a pillow had long since been over-turned. But Jacob found it again and lifted it up. Then, with his sons gathered about him, he related what had happened there thirty years before and the vow that he had made, and how God had answered him there in the day of his distress. Then he made his offering and sacrifice and worshiped God, and God appeared unto him again.

This story of Jacob and his dream at Bethel, and his broken vow, and then the fulfillment of it thirty years after, often comes back to me at the Easter season; for I think of many who were once at their Bethel, but have wandered far from it—once in close friendship with God, but now almost strangers to him—and yet who, on this Sunday, perhaps, have a fleeting vision of what they saw at Bethel, a wistful yearning to return, and are hearing a voice that bids them come. Perhaps for the first time in many years there may be stirring in their breasts a true Christian desire. Chords long silent have begun to vibrate again. I speak to them; and even those who have tried to keep close to their Bethel will profit by a call to come back to it.

ALL MEN HAVE A BETHEL IN THEIR LIFE

By that I mean some conviction or vision of heavenly things, perhaps a sacred vow that they made with themselves and with God. The religious instinct may be suppressed, but it is ineradicable and indestructible. The folk who live on the shores of Brittany have their beautiful tradition of the fabled city of Is. According to the story, Is was a large and populous city which one day sank suddenly beneath the waves of the sea; but there are times when the fisherman plying his trade will see the tips of the spires of the lost city appear for a little above the surface of the sea when the sun is shining brightly, and times when the peasants who live on the cliffs of Brittany can hear the pealing of the bells of the churches of the buried city. A man's religious life may be—alas, often is—sadly submerged, covered with the flotsam and jetsam, the debris and wreckage of this world; but the instinct of it still is there, and now and then that life and that desire will declare itself.

Childhood certainly had its Bethel. Childhood,

before the face has hardened and the soul has been encrusted with the long tragedy of life, is a time when it is easy to see the angels with the ladders. The last time I was at Baalbek, that most imposing and most stupendous monument of the ancient world, I recalled Thomas Moore's story of *Paradise and the Peri*. The Peri had been promised that she could get back into Paradise if she brought to the gates of heaven that which was most precious to God. All over the world she searched for that treasure. She brought first the last drop of blood from a dying patriot's heart, and then a maiden's kiss of sacrificial love implanted on the brow of her dying lover. But the gates of heaven opened not. Her gifts were refused. Then near the ruins of Baalbek she saw a child kneeling in prayer by a fountain. As the child was praying, a man rode up on his horse and dismounted to quench his thirst at the fountain. On his face was stamped all manner of iniquity and coarseness and crime. But as he stooped to lift the water to his lips, he saw the child kneeling in prayer. In a moment the hard face softened and changed, and a tear flowed down his cheek, for he recalled the day when he too was as innocent as the child, and prayed for himself as the child was now praying. It was that penitential tear that opened the gates of Paradise to the lost spirit.

How true, for so many of us, are those words of Thomas Hood:

> I remember, I remember
> The fir-trees dark and high;
> I used to think their slender tops
> Were close against the sky:
> It was a childish ignorance,
> But now 'tis little joy
> To know I'm farther off from Heaven
> Than when I was a boy.

A number of years ago a young man was coming from California to visit the East. In the Pullman car with him were three or four race-track gamblers. They were rough, hardened, godless, but somewhat interesting men; and this young man, who himself had been wandering from the training of his youth, was soon on familiar terms with them. At a town on the way a little boy was put on the car and given over to the custody of the Pullman conductor. When night came the porter made up the berth for the boy. The gamblers and this young man were sitting across the aisle from the boy's berth. Presently the boy came out in his nightdress and, looking at first timidly up and down the aisle, knelt down to say his prayers. At once those gamblers ceased their loud conversation and removed their hats in reverential pose. The young man himself felt a lump in his throat as he looked at the praying child. What had happened? The prayer of a child had carried them all back to their Bethel. The young man afterwards entered the ministry and became a well-known preacher of the Gospel. Thus was fulfilled the saying of the Bible, "And a little child shall lead them."

Sometimes men have been at their Bethel and felt a godly desire in their hearts when they awakened to the sacred greatness of life. And how much there is of that, after all—that longing for a better life amid the muck and the mire of this world. Perhaps that desire was awakened at a marriage altar, by an infant's smile, or a mother's deathbed. Or Bethel may have come, as it did in the case of Jacob, in some moment of awakening conscience, in the hour of distress or danger, in the hour of deliverance from death when the shadow ran back on the face of the dial. Then it was easy to vow and easy to promise to serve the Lord.

WANDERING FROM BETHEL

It is just as easy today to get far away from Bethel, away down into the Mesopotamia and the Shechem of sin, as it was in the days of Jacob. In the battle of life, holy impressions fade. There are plenty of men today who could hardly be recognized as the men their friends saw ten, twenty, thirty years ago. The ladder and the angels have faded away; the shields of gold have been traded for the

[119]

shields of brass. Are there any men or women like that among you? Tell me, did not I see thee once at Bethel? Did not I see thee vow at the altar? Did not I hear thy vow?

RETURNING TO BETHEL

God cares as much for you and for me as he did for Jacob, and he speaks as earnestly to you as he did to Jacob.

If you are going to get back to Bethel, God must first of all speak to you. There can be no start towards Bethel without that. The world will never tell you to go back, for the world's business is to keep a man as far as possible from Bethel. Your friends may think of it, and perhaps wish it, but they will rarely speak of it. Only God's voice, only the Holy Spirit, ever says, "Arise, go up to Bethel." Perhaps that is what he is saying now to some soul, "Arise, go up to Bethel."

With obedience to that voice there must be sacrifice. Jacob did not try to take his idols back to Bethel with him; and if you are going back to God, do not try to take your idols with you. Are you willing to bury them? I would not call you to Bethel under false pretenses. I would not tell you to come into the church without any cost or sacrifice in the way of burying idols. Are there associations, or pleasures, or comforts, or games, or dislikes, or enmities, or habits which stand between you and Bethel and which ought to be buried?

When you come back you can count on God's welcome. When Jacob returned to Bethel and fulfilled his vow, God was there to meet him and bless him again. Oh, wonderful, marvelous, patient, kind, all-loving, all-seeking, all-forgiving love of God in Christ! Yes! He is there to meet you when you come back. The past shall be forgotten. Jacob wandered from God; but when God called him and he came back to Bethel God appeared to him again and blessed him. David wandered from God and fell into the deepest sin; but when God spake to him through the prophet and called him back, and David repented and came, God was there to meet him when he came. Peter fell and wandered from God when he denied his Lord with an oath; but when Jesus looked upon him, and Peter repented and came back on that first resurrection Sabbath, Christ was there to meet him and bless him. The dying thief wandered from God; but when he repented and came back, Christ met him on the Cross and took him, first of all saved souls, into the Kingdom of Heaven with him. Yes! God is waiting for you. For some of you he has been waiting a long time. Will you arise and go unto him?

THE NIGHT OF THE TEMPEST

"Peace, be still."

"THEY THAT GO DOWN TO THE SEA IN SHIPS, THAT do business in great waters; these see the works of the Lord, and his wonders in the deep." That was what the disciples of Jesus were to see that night as they went down with him to the sea in ships.

The Jewish rabbis used to say that God created all the seas, but that the Sea of Galilee was his chosen one. It is, indeed, a chosen sea. It is a beautiful body of water, as beautiful as unique. Oval in shape and thirteen miles long by seven wide, surrounded by the brown mountains that rise as high as two thousand feet on the eastern shores, it makes one think of a sapphire stone set in gold. Away to the north, towers the ever-snow-capped summit of Mount Hermon.

It is a "chosen sea," too, because of the great part it plays in the life of our Lord. As to other places in the sacred narrative, Calvary, Gethsemane, the Sepulcher, one cannot be certain. Some of these places with their polyglot humanity and offensively bedizened shrines offend the sensibility of the pious

[122]

pilgrim who would walk in the footsteps of his Lord. But the Sea of Galilee rolls just as it did in the days of our Lord. The fishermen still sail their boats and ply their nets on its surface; the same brown mountains rise above it; the same stars look down upon it; the same storms convulse its bosom.

Take out of the New Testament the incidents in the life of Jesus associated with the Sea of Galilee, and a good part of the Gospels is gone. There at Capernaum he made his home; there he worked many of his greatest miracles; there he called his disciples; there he preached some of his greatest sermons; there he walked on the sea and stilled the tempest; and there he appeared unto his disciples after his resurrection.

The strain of preaching, physical, mental, spiritual, is intense. All day Jesus had been teaching and preaching to the people. He had told them the great Parable of the Sower and other parables and sermons, his pulpit the bow of a fisherman's boat. Now at eventide, weary and done out, he says to his disciples, "Let us pass over to the other side." They agree at once, and, says Mark, "took him even as he was"—that is, without any extra baggage, or another cloak, but "even as he was." You can see him as he steps over the thwarts of the ship and lies down in the broad seat at the stern. His head rests on a piece of sailcloth, or a wet coil of the nets, for a pillow, and almost immediately he falls asleep. One of the disciples, probably Peter, holding to the bow of the boat, gives it a shove down the gravelly beach, and then leaps into it as it reaches deep water. The black horizontal sail is hoisted and the course set for the hills of Gadara, dimly outlined on the eastern horizon. It is a perfect night; the stars are shining, and the soft wind is filling out the sail. Jesus is calmly sleeping, his respiration in rhythm with the pulsation of the sea. There is no sound, save the low voices of the apostles and the gentle slap of the water against the bow of the ship as it plows through the sea. Someone has thrown a mantle over Christ, and not far from him, I am sure, sits John, his beloved disciple. All around them, too, are "other little ships," part of the same flotilla bound for the eastern shore.

THE STORM

Like life, the Sea of Galilee can be calm one moment and swept with gales the next. The sea lies in a basin six hundred feet below the level of the Mediterranean. The colder winds, rushing down from the mountains and the uplands, roaring down through the gorges as if through a funnel, meet the warmer air in the basin of the sea and there is convulsion and commotion.

So it was this night. Andrew said to Peter, "It looks as if we would have a bit of a blow tonight." And Peter said to Andrew, "It does look a little like it. Perhaps we had better shorten sail." But before they can do that the hurricane is upon them. The sail cracks like the report of a pistol. The next moment sail and mast are swept overboard by the rush of the wind. Now the sea, obedient to its master, the wind, begins to rage. On every side, port and starboard, fore and aft, the great waves come rushing in and smash against the sides of the ship, sometimes sweeping over it. Since most of the disciples were seasoned navigators on the Sea of Galilee, and they were all frightened, it must have been a storm indeed!

The waves rise higher and higher. All the stars are extinguished. The lightning flashes; the thunder crashes; and the rain falls like a cataract. The disciples see Jesus as he lies sleeping in the stern of the boat, now far above their heads as the ship pitches, and then far beneath them as the stern sinks into the trough of a wave. Yet he sleeps on. How different from the sleep of Jonah! Jonah slept because his conscience was dead; Jesus because of a good conscience. Jonah was the cause of the storm that shook his vessel; but Jesus was the secret of the deliverance of his ship from destruction. So he sleeps.

This is the only time we see Jesus sleeping. At other times we see him teaching, preaching, rejoicing, walking, resting, eating, drinking, praying, agonizing, dying. This is the only time we see him sleeping. Sleep on, Master! Thy Spirit is willing, but, as with us, thy flesh is sometimes weary. Sleep on, with that fisherman's net for thy pillow, and the winds and the waves, so fearsome to thy disciples, only a lullaby for thee who commandest the sea and the stormy winds.

The frightened disciples debate as to whether to waken Jesus. At length one, shaking him by the shoulder, cries, "Master, carest thou not that we perish?"

What a subject for a great artist, the awakened Jesus standing majestic in the stern of the ship. First he spoke to the elements. He looked up and rebuked the wind, and it folded its wings. He looked down and rebuked the sea, and the waves fell flat on their faces. And there was a great calm. Then he spoke to the disciples. "Why are ye so fearful? how is it that ye have no faith?"

THE POWER OF CHRIST

While they continued in safety to the other shore, and all the other little boats with them, the disciples said one to another, "What manner of man is this, that even the wind and the sea obey him?" That was the very lesson that Jesus wanted to teach his disciples, and, through them, wants to teach us—that he is the kind of a Man who has power to make the wind and the sea obey him.

As the storm that night broke over the placid Sea of Galilee, so storms break suddenly over the soul on life's voyage to the other side. But the same Christ who stilled the tempest that night is able to command the winds and the waves that agitate our lives.

What is it that makes the storm? Nothing but the wind. If the wind never rose, the sea would always be calm. It is when the winds blow that the waves rise, and when the wind goes down the waves go down too. Thus the winds that bring the storms at sea are like those circumstances and events and incidents in life which produce waves of agitation and distress in the soul. But He who quelled the tempest that night on the Sea of Galilee is able to still every storm that sweeps over your soul.

After all, the disciples did the wise thing, the only thing, that night, when they awakened Jesus. In the storms that sweep over the soul that is always the thing to do. Awaken the Christ who is never far from you, but who, too often, sleeps within thy soul.

THE TEMPEST OF FEAR

This may take the form of anxiety or worry and

care. How common a storm that is in life. How many souls there are in stormy agitation. Some are concerned about earthly possessions: economic storms threaten to sweep everything away and leave them in dependency. Some are worried about the body: there are intimations of declining health. Some are anxious about the welfare of those they love: mothers and fathers today think of their sons in the armed forces, and the great danger that confronts them. But from all these fears there is a deliverance. Awaken the sleeping Christ! Call on him! Call upon Christ when the tempest of fear and anxiety agitates your soul, and hear him say to the winds and the waves, "Peace, be still!"

THE STORM OF SORROW AND BEREAVEMENT

This storm breaks as suddenly as that on Gennesaret's erstwhile placid face. Suddenly the soft south wind becomes a gale. The gentle waves are raging; the stars' familiar faces have gone out, and you are alone in the night on the sea, in the storm. What then? Only one thing! Awaken the Christ who sleeps within you. Paul speaks of those who sorrow as those who have no hope. That means those who have no Christ. But you have a Christ! If you do not, you can have him. Call on him. Learn his faithful and tender love. Hear his voice speaking to the tempest of your sorrow, "Peace, be still!"

THE STORM OF ANGER AND INNER TURMOIL

Someone has hurt you, irritated you, wounded you, insulted you, wronged you, lied about you. You are all stirred up within, agitated and angry. Nothing for the moment can please you or divert you, for your mind keeps reverting to this one thing, which cancels all the satisfactions of life. What then? Instead of acting on the impulse of the moment and giving vent to your anger and wrath and resentment, try the method of the disciples. Call on Jesus! Awaken him! Hear him speak to the tempest of your anger, "Peace, be still!" Then, when the calm comes, you will wonder at your former distress and agitation.

THE TEMPEST OF DOUBT

O could we make our doubts remove,
  Those gloomy doubts which rise.

Sometimes the sky of our faith is clouded. We look over the world today and see everywhere "garments rolled in blood" and the Horsemen of Death, like the locusts of the abyss, going forth to torment, not a third part of the earth, but the whole world. We sometimes wonder, too, about the moral government of the world, and the great truths of Divine

Revelation—that God has visited our world, that he died for it on the cross, and that there is a life after death. Or it may be a question as to the goodness of God in the providence of our own life. Then we may be tempted to say what the disciples said that night, "Carest thou not that we perish?" In that hour do what the disciples did: awaken the Christ that sleeps within you. Learn how much he cares; hear that voice speaking through your tempest, "Peace, be still!"

THE STORM OF TEMPTATION

Here is a storm that sweeps over every scene. Sometimes it breaks as suddenly as the storm did that night on the starlit face of Tiberias. First, there is a soft wind that draws the soul on and tempts it with its false promises, as the soft wind did Paul's ship that day off the coast of Crete. Then comes the quick and sudden change. Now it is not a soft and beguiling south wind, but the roar and sweep of the tempest. All that you have planned for, hoped for, prayed for, seems to be in danger, and *is* in danger, and will be sunk and lost unless you can call on Christ who is able and willing to deliver, far beyond all that you can ask or think. Speak to him! Awaken the Christ that sleeps within you. He still knows how to cast out the evil spirits. Hear him rebuke them and drive them from your soul, as he says, "Peace, be still!" Then comes the calm. Then you know that you are safe. Then come the angels to minister to you, as they came and ministered to Christ after Satan had departed from him.

THE STORM OF REMORSE AND GUILT AND SORROW FOR SIN

The Bible talks about sowing the wind and reaping the whirlwind. That is the kind of storm about which I am talking now. There is no storm that excites the soul as that. It is the storm of conscience. Conscience heaves the soul as the tide heaves the face of the ocean. Who can minister to the conscience smitten? Who can stay the winds and the waves of sin? Only One. And that is what Christ came to do. He is the Prince of Peace—the peace of forgiveness, the peace of reconciliation. Call on him, and see him lift his hands and say to that storm of sin and guilt, "Peace, be still! Go in peace; thy sins are forgiven thee!"

Perhaps there are some of you who in a particular way need to hear that voice of Christ. And all of us, no doubt, may well ask for more of his peace and calm. One of these tempests of which I have been speaking may be agitating you—fear, care, worry, sorrow, anger, doubt, temptation, and sin. Will you now call on him? Lift up your hand and touch him. Awaken him, as his disciples lifted their hand and lifted their voice to awaken him that night. He is still able to do it. The winds and the waves still obey his voice. He is still able to say, he is still willing to say, "Peace, be still!"

X

THE NIGHT OF NIGHTS

> "And there were in the same country
> shepherds abiding in the field, keeping watch
> over their flock by night."
>
> LUKE 2:8

THIS WAS THE NIGHT OF NIGHTS! YET THAT
Night of Nights came down as all other nights had
come down before, thousands upon thousands, ever
since the first day came to a close and the first sun
sank beyond the horizon, and God divided the light
and the darkness, and called the light day and the
darkness called he night.

The Night of Nights has come. And yet it came
just as every other night before it had come. Toward the west, toward the Mediterranean Sea, the
sun began to sink. Lower and lower it sank, until
across the border of the western sky was one great
bar of gold. Then that path of gold turned to blood
red, flushing all the sky with crimson and touching
earth with its fire. But in a moment the sky, so red
with glory, turned to a cold ashen gray; and after
that came night. To the east the mountains of
Moab rise out of the shadows like colossal giants.
In Bethlehem's houses mothers lay their children
down to sleep. In the courtyards of the inn the

[133]

camels and the cattle have lain down to rest. Here and there in some of the houses lights gleam for a moment and then go out. In the fields the sheep lie down while the shepherds sit about their fire. In the heavens above appear the same stars that had shone through all the ages, ever since God made the "stars to rule by night." Orion weaves his mystic band of Light, and the Pleiades, to the unheard music of the spheres, commence their march across the heavens.

Night had come down, just the same as night had come down in all the centuries before. Yet this is the Night of Nights! This is the night that will conquer darkness and bring in the day when there shall be night no more. This is the night when they who sit in darkness shall see a great light. This is the night that shall make eternal light, for it is the night when God brought into the world Him who is the Light of the world. Yonder, in that stable of the inn, where the cattle are breathing softly in their slumber, a virgin mother has brought forth her child and laid him in a manger. The cattle heeded it not; but over that Bethlehem manger a Star will halt and angels will sing. The long journey of preparation for the redemption of the world ends on this Night of Nights. Immanuel has come!

"There were . . . . shepherds abiding in the field, keeping watch over their flock by night." The first message came to those shepherds. Not to the kings and potentates of the earth, not to the conquering soldiers, not to the rich and powerful and learned of the world, but to those shepherds as they kept watch over their flocks by night was the first Christmas sermon preached and the great tidings brought unto them that a Saviour was born.

Sometimes the preacher will feel that the best he can do is to bow down in adoration before the Child, as those shepherds did, and listen to the holy song of the heavenly host, "Glory to God in the highest, and on earth peace, good will toward men!" No Christmas sermon will ever improve upon that; for in that chorus of the angels is summed up all the glory, all the beauty, and all the power of Christ and his redemption.

Poetical Luke wrote, "As the angels were gone away from them into heaven, the shepherds said one to another, Let us now go even unto Bethlehem, and see this thing which is come to pass, which the Lord hath made known unto us." Suppose we talk to ourselves with the same words and with the same music. Forget, if you can, and if you will, your sad memories, your fears, your anxieties, your distresses, your worldly thoughts and ambitions and purposes, and, as the shepherds said, "Let us now go even unto Bethlehem, and see this thing which is come to pass, which the Lord hath made known unto us."

THE PROPHECY AND THE PREPARATION OF THE INCARNATION

The great event of this Night of Nights came not without preparation, or predication and promise. In the very beginning, after the fall of man, rang out over the fallen race the first note of the Gospel, the somewhat vague and dim, yet certain, promise of a Deliverer and Saviour, that the seed of the woman should bruise the head of the serpent. To Abraham the promise was given that through his descendants all nations of the earth should be blessed. Moses tells the people that a greater law-giver than he will appear in the future. Balaam, a prophet and seer outside Israel, in the rapture of his vision declares, "There shall come a Star out of Jacob, and a Sceptre shall rise out of Israel." The Psalmist sings of a great King whose name shall endure forever, and who shall have the heathen for his inheritance and the uttermost parts of the earth for his possession. The prophets declare that the Desire of the Nations shall come, and that "his name shall be called Wonderful, Counsellor, The mighty God, The everlasting Father, The Prince of Peace." In addition to these general promises and predictions there is much that is more specific. The One who is to come will be of the tribe of Judah, of the line of David, and Bethlehem will be his birthplace. His coming will be preceded by the advent of a great prophet who shall prepare the way for him by the preaching of repentance. Thus the Gulf Stream of Old Testament prophecy washed the shores of the remotest ages and prepared the way for the coming of the Saviour.

Why did Christ not come one hundred or ten hundred years before he did, or one hundred or ten hundred years after he did? The answer is that he came in "the fulness of the time," when the time was ripe, at the end of the period of preparation. "God takes a step, and the ages have elapsed."

There was a fullness of preparation among the Jewish people. In Abraham God divided the river of humanity into two streams, which flow separately until they meet again in Christ. The Jewish law proclaimed the oneness and the holiness of God. The Tabernacle and the Temple sacrifices were the shadows of the great Sacrifice of Christ upon the Cross. When the apostles went forth to preach Christ and him crucified, wherever they went they found scattered colonies of the dispersed Jewish people, and the Jewish synagogue was the first Christian pulpit. Although Christ came to his own and his own received him not, yet there were those who were expecting him and waiting for him, like the devout Simeon, who waited "for the consolation of Israel." It was not by accident, then, that on this Night of Nights the Saviour was born in Bethlehem of Judea, instead of at Athens or in Rome.

There was a fullness of preparation, too, in the heathen or Gentile world. The world had failed by wisdom to know God, and had confessed that failure. One of the noblest of pagan writers, Plato, said that man must take his own reason and use it as a raft on which to pass through the stormy seas, until a revelation shall come. At the time the Child was born at Bethlehem, pagan morals had sunk into a fearful climax of iniquity and shame, when men "changed the truth of God into a lie, and worshipped and served the creature more than the Creator." A dying, poisoned, hopeless world was ready for the Gospel of life and forgiveness and righteousness and hope.

The conquests of Alexander the Great had given the world an almost universal tongue, and that speech was ready for those who proclaimed and wrote the Gospel. The conquests of Rome had crushed the warring and independent nations of the world, and the Roman peace reigned when Christ was born. Otherwise, humanly speaking, Christianity would have been strangled in its cradle. But under the aegis of Roman law and government and

over the splendid Roman highways the heralds of
the Gospel went forth to preach Christ and him
crucified. Now had come the set time. God's hour
had struck. Upon the men of that day had come the
"end of the ages." Halt, Holy, Sacred Star, over
Bethlehem's manger, for the long process of preparation has come to an end, and the world is ready for
the angel's song!

THE MANNER OF THE INCARNATION

What we have here is not the story of a God
who appeared on earth, and not the story of a man
lifted up to godhead, but that God became man, that
the Eternal Word became flesh and dwelt among us.
This is a stupendous fact, the most overwhelming
fact that can be presented to human intelligence.
Even the great mind of Paul when he pondered it,
exclaimed, "Great is the mystery of godliness: God
was manifest in the flesh."

In the Gospels of Matthew and Luke we have the
sublime story of how he came. God not only sent
his only begotten Son into the world, but sent him
in a way which forever touches and thrills the heart
of man. It was a way which will make all nations
and all ages celebrate it to the end of time. There
are, indeed, some today who claim to know better
than God himself how God ought to have come, and
who say he did not come in the way the Gospels tell

us he did come, conceived by the Holy Ghost and born of the Virgin Mary. The sublime narrative of the virgin birth of our Lord is a touchstone, as it were, of men's faith. The discounting or denial of the virgin birth of our Lord is inevitably linked with that indifference and coldness and dead secularism and passionless unbelief which rest as a blight upon so many of the churches and have taken the ring out of the voice of so many pulpits.

Christianity depends upon its great facts. It cannot be ethically and morally true, and at the same time historically false. In the virgin birth of our Lord we have the constituent miracle of the Christian faith. It is, indeed, a supreme and stupendous miracle, but not more so than God himself, not more so than the soul of man, not more so than the Holy Spirit, and not more so than the Atonement on the Cross, or the Resurrection of Christ from the dead. Without this record of his birth, Christ would be the supreme enigma of the ages.

We rejoice that he came in the way that he did. All the sweet winsomeness and charm of the Christmas story gathers about his birth, the way in which he came: the Star leading on the philosophers from the East; the wondering and musings of the guileless maid of Nazareth at what the angel had told her; the virgin mother overtaken in her great hour at Bethlehem, where there was no room for them in the inn; the manger cradle; the lowing cattle; the bowing shepherds; the echoing song of the angels. Yes, let the Star shine! Who would put it out? Let the Angel of the Lord speak to Joseph and Mary and Elisabeth and the shepherds! Who would silence his voice? Let the philosophers from the East bow down with their gifts of gold and frankincense and myrrh! Who would send them away? Let the shepherds bow at the cradle and adore! Who would stop them? Let the multitude of the heavenly host sing their holy song of good will to man and peace on earth and glory to God in the highest! Who would silence their singing?

THE PURPOSE AND THE POWER OF THE INCARNATION

We are not left in doubt as to the purpose of that wonderful birth on that Night of Nights in Bethlehem's cradle. The prophets of old tell us that he will come as a Saviour and to establish the Kingdom of Redemption. The Angel of the Lord said to Joseph that his name was to be Jesus, because he will save his people from their sins. The Angel of the Lord told the shepherds that unto them a Saviour was born; and the song that the angels sang that night has been telling the world ever since that Christ was born that God might be glorified and that he came to bring peace to the souls of men.

John said that he came to bring light and life into the world. Paul said that he came to save sinners; and Jesus himself, the Child who was born, summed it all up by saying that he came to "seek and to save that which was lost," and that "God so loved the world, that he gave his only begotten Son, that whosoever believeth in him should not perish, but have everlasting life." The Child that was born on this Night of Nights was born to die upon the Cross for man's salvation. Through his birth and through his death he came to seek and to save that which was lost. And through all the ages Christ has been seeking and has been finding the lost. A light was kindled in the world that night, and ever since men who sat in darkness have seen a great light. The storms and clouds of the centuries have never been able to put it out; and still, through the dark, sad clouds of man's anarchy and sin and passion and war shines softly and beautifully, and with invincible hope, the Everlasting Light.

Christ came to bestow religious peace—peace between God and man, the peace of forgiveness—not political peace. But if all men were to receive that peace, we would have peace between the nations also. Of all the stirring, dramatic events of World War I, the one that I remember most is an event that took place on the first Christmas of that dreadful war. After months of unavailing slaughter, the colossal

armies of the German Empire and France and Great
Britain had fought themselves to a standstill, and
now millions of their soldiers were glaring at one
another out of the trenches that gashed the earth
from the North Sea clear to the Alps.

In Flanders the German army lay confronting the
British army. All about them the desolate, bleak
country was strewn with the wreckage of the terrible
struggle of these armies—blackened and ruined villages and smashed churches; jagged trunks of trees,
cut down by the artillery; and everywhere a sea of
yellow mud. Everywhere, too, were the dead—the
dead of a month ago, the dead of a week ago, the
dead of yesterday, the dead of last night. The dead
were buried in the parapets of the trenches where
the soldiers stood. They lay strewn in dreadful
litter over No Man's Land, and clung like scarecrows
to the barbed-wire defenses of both armies.

Then came Christmas Eve, the Night of Nights,
the night on which our Saviour was born. Standing
on their platforms in the hostile trenches, the men
in gray and the men in khaki watched for an attack
of the enemy. But no attack came that night. At
length the night passed, and the December sun rose.
It was Christmas Day, the day of our Saviour, the
day of the Prince of Peace. At stand-to in the
morning, the British soldiers on the alert held their
rifles with numb fingers and waited and watched, the

frost and steam from their breath rising like a cloud on the cold winter air. Every morning they had heard a hymn of hate from the German trenches in the loud music of a burst of artillery fire. But this morning the hymn of hate did not rise. The guns back of the German trenches were silent. A great stillness came down over both lines of battle. What was to happen that Christmas morning? Suddenly the British soldiers saw three gray-clad soldiers rise out of the German trenches. This time they came without bayonets or hand grenades. Slowly, cautiously, and at first with pathetic hesitation, they approached and passed the line of their own barbed wire, and stood unprotected in No Man's Land. In a moment, before the officers realized what was happening, men by the hundreds were scrambling out of the German trenches and the British trenches, and running forward into No Man's Land.

The mud of Flanders had covered the German gray and the British khaki alike, and given to all a common uniform. The soldiers who yesterday were seeking to kill one another now put out their hands in friendly clasp and greeting, and wished one another in broken English and in broken German a Merry Christmas. Then songs were called for. The Germans responded with "Die Wacht am Rhine," and the English with "Tipperary," and the Scotch with "The Boys of Bonnie Scotland." Then the

Germans began to sing, "Heilige Nacht," and "O Tannenbaum!" and the English answered with the Christmas songs of England. So passed the morning and the afternoon of Christmas Day in brotherly friendship and mutual songs and the exchanging of gifts. Then the light of Christmas Day faded, and the men in gray and the men in khaki went back to their dismal trenches and took up once more the instruments of death.

Only an interlude, that was, in the chorus of war; only one incident on that far-flung battle line. But it was one of those incidents which create hope within the breast of man, which make us believe, in spite of the clouds of war and hatred that now infest our planet, that love is stronger than hate, that light is stronger than darkness, and that with the birth of Christ there came into the world a power which shall one day overcome the powers of darkness and bring in everlasting light and everlasting peace.

And, wonder of wonders, this Night of Nights was for you alone! Had you been the only one astray from God, had you been the only one who needed a Saviour, still the Night of Nights would have come. Still Christ would have been born, and still Christ would have died for you on Calvary. Will you go now with the shepherds to Bethlehem and bow before this Christ? Will you receive him as your King and Saviour? There are many who still reject him, as they did when Christ first came. But to as many as received him, to them gives he power to become the sons of God. Think of that! To become the sons of God! Power over sorrow, power over time, power over hate, power over temptation, power over sin, power over death!

XI

THE NIGHT SHOUTS ROUTED AN ARMY

> "So Gideon, and the hundred men that
> were with him, came unto the outside of the
> camp in the beginning of the middle watch;
> . . . . and they cried, The sword of the Lord,
> and of Gideon."
>
> JUDGES 7:19-20

TOWARD THE WEST THE SUN WAS DROPPING SLOWLY like a great red ball into the Mediterranean. Here on the top of a flat rock on Mount Gilboa two men are stretched out at full length, watching the camp of the invading army of the Midianites, which is spread out across the valley of Esdraelon. That famous valley is the most fought-over soil on this earth, from the time of Sisera and Barak to the day of Gideon, and from the day of Gideon to the age of Elijah, and from the age of Elijah to the time of Saul and Jonathan, who fell on Mount Gilboa. In that valley Josiah fought at Megiddo with Pharaoh-Necho. There the Crusaders fought the Moslems; there Napoleon fought the Turks; there the British army under Allenby fought against the same Turks. No wonder that John, in his inspired picture of the last great battle, stages that battle at Armageddon, or the Hill of Megiddo, in the valley of Esdraelon.

From their mountain outpost these two men of the army of Israel can see far beneath them the camp of the Midianites: the black tents of the soldiers; the spacious pavilions of the commanding officer, with their standards floating over them; the herds of camels and horses; the stir and bustle about the campfires as the soldiers prepare for their supper. Now and then the evening wind carries up from the valley the neigh of one of the war horses, or the blare of a trumpet. But now the sun has set and night comes on quickly. The brown mountains begin to fade into gray and black. In the camp can be seen only an occasional flash of a torch or the glow of the embers of a campfire. The stir of war, the sounds of revelry and debauchery in the camp give way to quiet and silence as man and beast sink down into sleep. Even the guards and sentinels slumber, for what, think they, has their great army to fear from the contemptible army of the Israelites?

Now the two men rise out of their hiding place on the rock and quickly, but cautiously, descend the mountainside into the midst of the camp of the Midianites. Soon they are on the outskirts of the heathen hosts, where they can hear the occasional barking of dogs, or the jingle of a camel's bell, or smell the reek of the camels. Once a rock, loosened by one of their feet, went tumbling down the moun-

tainside toward the camp, and the two men halted
in fear lest the noise should betray their presence.
Once one of them stumbled over the neck of a sleeping camel. But finally they get right up against the
camp and take their station close against the black
tent in which two Midianite soldiers are sleeping.
There they lie, eager and attentive, not daring even
to whisper one to the other, and almost hearing their
hearts beat with excitement. Within the tent one
of the men stirs uneasily and, awakening his companion, says: "Behold, I dreamed a dream, and, lo
. . . ." But before we tell that dream let us go back to
the beginning of the story and see what led up to the
dream.

GIDEON'S CALL

Under an oak in Ophrah, on a hidden wine press,
a stalwart young Hebrew is beating out the wheat,
the few lean ears he had managed to grow and har-
vest in some ravine where the Midianites had not
yet penetrated. As he thus flails the grain, his
fine brow dark with resentment, and his manly eye
kindling with patriotic fire as he looks off toward the
distant valley where the army of Midian is en-
camped, the angel of the Lord appears unto him
and says: "The Lord is with thee, thou mighty man
of valour." But Gideon, for that was the young
man's name, wonders whether that is so or not.
"If the Lord be with us, why then is all this be-

fallen us? And where be all his miracles which our
fathers told us of, saying, Did not the Lord bring
us up from Egypt? but now the Lord hath forsaken
us, and delivered us into the hands of the Midianites."

How old that kind of religious trouble and doubt
is! Men of today look back to the days of the
apostles, and wonder why God is not with his Church
in mighty pentecostal blessings as he was in that
great day. Where are the miracles with which
Christ certified his divine authority? In the days
of the apostles men must have looked back to the
age of the great prophets and longed for a demon-
stration of the divine power such as was granted unto
them; and in the age of the great prophets men must
have looked back to the age of the patriarchs, as
Gideon here looked back to the day of Israel's deliverance from the land of Egypt and the house of
bondage. It is common to think that yesterday was
a better day than today, and that God did greater
things for the men who served him generations ago
than he does for us today. Yet faith in God lives
on, and shall live, because in his own way God gives
us evidence that he is, and that he is a hearer of
prayer, and that his arm is not shortened that it
cannot save.

In answer to Gideon's troubled question, the angel
first of all *"looked"* upon Gideon. There was elo-

quent speech in that look, for sometimes one look can be the greatest speech. A look can say, can tell, what even words cannot tell. How much more than words there was in that "look" of our Lord when he turned and "looked upon Peter," after he had heard him deny him and curse him in the court-yard of the high priest! That "look" which the angel gave Gideon was the look of a commission, the look of a charge. It said to Gideon, "Thou art the man! Thou art able to do this! God will be with thee." It is said of Napoleon that when he took his officers by the hand at the beginning of a battle and looked on them they felt like conquerors. So God looks upon you and me. He has made us for himself. The divine element is in your soul. You can do his will. You can do his work in the world. You can become, if you will, a man after God's own heart. O Angel of the Lord, look on me!

The various signs which Gideon asks of the Lord do not show a fearful heart or a doubting heart, but a great desire to be sure that God is with him. On both occasions the angel grants his request and gives him a sign: first the fire that rose up out of the rock and consumed the flesh and the unleavened bread; and then the beautiful sign of the fleece and the dew—now the fleece wet with dew and the ground dry, and now the ground wet with dew, but the fleece dry.

GIDEON'S WAR

True service for God on the part of the Church must commence with reformation within the Church. Gideon was oppressed with the burden of Israel's enslavement under the hated Midianites, and when God called him he told him that he was to deliver Israel from the hand of the Midianites. That was a task to fire the imagination of any man of faith and valor. But there was to be a prelude to that great act of deliverance, and that prelude probably took more faith and more courage than did the campaign against the armies of Midian.

Israel was not only enslaved, but degraded. Her abject political and national estate was God's punishment upon the people for their idolatry. Even Gideon's household had succumbed to the universal corruption, and his own father, Joash, had by his house a grove and altar to Baal. As Gideon prepares himself to sound the trumpet and march against the enemies of the country, the angel of the Lord tells him to march first against the grove and idol in his father's house. That took courage of the highest sort. But the thing was done. This first battle of Gideon, as the last, was a night battle. In the night the axes rang against the trunks of the trees in the grove, and the young bullock and the ten men with Gideon pulled Baal off his pedestal and left him lying on his face in prostrate ignominy. In the morning the men of the city came and demanded that Joash put his son to death for this act of sacrilege towards Baal. But Joash was secretly glad that the thing had been done, and that his house had been cleared of idolatry, and pointedly he told the mob that surged about his home that if Baal was a god he could plead for himself. And from that day they called Gideon "Jerubbaal," "Let Baal plead."

Do you wish to do something worth while for God, and make a witness for the truth? Which way will you march? Very likely the first thing for you is to do some idol chopping in your own heart. Are there no secret sins? Are there no portions held back from God? Are there no dark chambers? Are there no rooms in your life where you stubbornly keep out the light? First put yourself right with God, and then God will use you as he sees fit.

When Gideon raised the standard of independence and blew the trumpet, the echoes of which thrilled every valley and glen of Israel, an army of thirty-two thousand men flocked to his standard, and he marched against the foe.

REDUCING THE ARMY

God looked this army over and said to Gideon, "Too many, Gideon; cut them down." The first test by which Gideon was directed to reduce his army was the test of fear. From their mountain encampment he let his army take one long look at the camp of the Midianites in the valley below them, their camels swarming like locusts, and the morning sun reflected from thousands upon thousands of burnished shields. "Whosoever is fearful and afraid, let him return." This was in keeping with the old law of Israel as recorded in the Book of Deuteronomy. Whenever the nation went out to war and the army was assembled, the officers were to say to the soldiers, "What man is there that is fearful and fainthearted? let him go and return unto his house, lest his brethren's heart faint as well as his heart." That was sound psychology, and also sound generalship. "Lest his brethren's heart faint as well as his heart." Better have a regiment of ten men full of resolution and courage than a regiment of one hundred men where ninety out of the hundred are afraid. An army is better off with the cowards out of its ranks than with them in it, no matter how numerous they are. This reduction of Gideon's army has its bearing upon the Church of Christ. A half believer, a man who fears the world more than he loves Christ, or a man whose life is unworthy of the Gospel, does more harm than good to the Church. Like the cowards in Israel's army, he infects others with his disease and may cause their hearts to melt.

How many do you think accepted the invitation of Gideon and took advantage of his offer to go back to their homes? Twenty-two thousand out of the thirty-two thousand! Gideon was left with an army of ten thousand. What was an army of ten thousand against the myriads of the Midianites? But now God tells him that his army is still too great, that it must be reduced by another test. The first test was that of courage. This second test is to be the test of earnestness and zeal.

Gideon was directed to march his army over a brook. To know what real thirst is, one must travel through the arid countries. Here was this army, heated with their march under the hot sun, coming down to one of the occasional brooks or streams. As they broke rank, ninety-seven hundred out of the ten thousand lay down on their bellies, and putting their mouths into the water like a horse or a cow, leisurely drank their fill. But three hundred, as they hurried through the stream, dashed the water up to their mouths with their hands. These were the men chosen for Gideon's final army. Their way of drinking showed earnestness and zeal in the cause in which they were enlisted. The other ninety-seven hundred by their manner of drinking at the brook showed that they thought more of satisfying their immediate thirst than they did of hastening forward to meet the foe. It seems like a strange proportion—ninety-seven hundred to three hundred. But still, in the organized army of Christ, the Church, the number of those who attend faithfully its services, engage in its work, and witness, and are zealous for its honor and for the Kingdom of Christ, are of the same proportion as the hand-lappers to the knee-drinkers in Gideon's army, or three hundred to ninety-seven hundred.

Apply this second test of indifference and carelessness, and you have once more cut down the army of the Church. Send back all those who do not care whether the Church stands by its faith or not; send home all those who do not care whether the Gospel is given to the heathen or not; send home those who never go to prayer meeting and never take the slightest part in the work of the Church; send home those who come only occasionally to the services of worship; send away those who spend the Sabbath day just as the worldling spends it—send home all these, and you have made a cut in the army like that which Gideon made in his. Yet the army will be stronger in the end.

I wonder what Gideon thought of his army now— this little handful of three hundred men? I think I can see him leaning on his sword as he stands on the top of that cliff overlooking the valley of Esdraelon. As the sun is going down towards Carmel and the sea, Gideon looks down upon the swarming hosts of the Midianites and the Amalekites, like grasshoppers for multitude. He can see the smoke going up from their campfires, the thousands of their camels, their shields and swords flashing in the sun, and he can hear the dim hum of their multitudinous voices. And this army he is to conquer with his three hundred men! We do not wonder that, without Gideon asking it, God encourages him with a sign.

The Lord said to Gideon, "Arise, get thee down unto the host; for I have delivered it into thine hand. . . . . And thou shalt hear what they say; and afterward shall thine hands be strengthened to go down unto the host." Gideon and his man-servant Phurah descend into the camp and secretly take their place under the fly of one of the black tents of Midian. That is where they were when they heard one of the soldiers relate the dream that troubled him. "Behold, I dreamed a dream, and, lo, a cake of barley bread tumbled into the host of Midian, and came unto a tent, and smote it that it fell, and overturned it, that the tent lay along." When his tentmate heard that dream, he said, "This is nothing else save the sword of Gideon . . . . for into his hand hath God delivered Midian, and all the host."

The moment Gideon heard that his heart leaped within him. Out of the mouth of the enemy himself he had heard the confirmation of what God had told him, that he would deliver the host of the Mid-

ianites into his hand. Putting out his hand to touch
Phurah, as a sign for him to follow, Gideon arose,
and carefully and cautiously made his way out of the
camp and up the mountain to where his three hundred men lay waiting. There, no longer doubting, he
said, "Arise; for the Lord hath delivered into your
hand the host of Midian!" With a trumpet in every
man's right hand, and a pitcher, with a lamp hid in
it, in the other hand, the three hundred stole down
to the edge of the Midianite camp. Then, when
Gideon gave the signal, there was the crash of three
hundred pitchers, the flashing and dancing of three
hundred torches and the blare of three hundred
trumpets. The startled host of the Midianites and
the Amalekites came tumbling out of their tents,
and in the darkness and confusion fell upon one another. When morning dawned upon the valley of
Esdraelon, it was strewn with the wreck of the invading army, clear to the fords of the Jordan, and
across the Jordan.

Like the leaves of the forest when Summer is green,
That host with their banners at sunset were seen:
Like the leaves of the forest when Autumn hath blown,
That host on the morrow lay withered and strown.[1]

GOD'S ENCOURAGEMENT

"Thou shalt hear what they say," God said to

[1] From "The Destruction of Sennacherib," by Lord Byron.

Gideon when he sent him down into the midst of the Midianites. "Thou shalt hear what they say!" Ah, we hear what they say—the world which the Church came to save. We hear what they are saying to us, what they say by way of challenge and derision, and scoffing and bitterness and doubt and criticism, but not what they say among themselves, what they say within their own hearts. Would that we might lie quietly by their tents and hear what they really think and say! Would that we might listen to their night thoughts! Could we only hear their words of anxious misgivings for the morrow of a life that knows not God; could we but see the restless tossing under the sting of remorse for sin; could we see their blank despair when the grave closes over one they love; could we hear what they say of a Christian character that has walked in their midst without guile or sin; could we catch the sigh of their wistful yearning after things pure and lasting; could we hear their secret verdict about the ultimate victory of the Kingdom of God, then, like Gideon, we should worship and return to our post full of hope, for we should know that the Lord is with us, and that the sword of the Lord is also the sword of the Church.

"Thou shalt hear what they say!" Here was a dream and a sign which strengthened resolution, confirmed hope, inspired victorious deeds. That is a dream that God sends not only to Gideon, but to all of us. He says, "Arise, get thee down unto the host; for I have delivered it into thine hand."

Are you battling with a temptation which you fear will overthrow you? Then hear the Word of the Lord: "Get thee down unto the host." You can conquer. Are you carrying a sorrow or a burden that seems too bitter or too heavy? You can bear it. Listen! I hear what is spoken in the deepest places of the soul. Thou art able to do it. Is it the renouncement or the abandonment of a great hope, or a fond desire? You are able for it. Hear what they say! Hear what the angels of the hosts of victory are proclaiming! Is it some cup of disappointment? You can drink it. You were down in the midst of the host this day, and you heard what they said. Is it a thorn in the flesh that pierces you? You are able to endure it, for thou shalt hear what others say who came off conquerors and more than conquerors.

The sword of the Lord is faith and trust in thy Saviour, Jesus Christ. In him you will conquer. I tell you, and I tell myself, for I have been down in the midst of the host; I have heard what they say. I have heard the enemies of thy soul acknowledge their defeat, for they know that Christ is with thee. I have seen thy name written on the scroll of the victors. "Arise, get thee down unto the host; for I have delivered it into thine hand!"

GIDEON'S FALL

You sometimes hear it said of certain noted men that if they had only died at this or that point in their great career it would have been far better for their fame. If Arnold had died at Quebec, or Saratoga! If David had died when he brought the Ark to Jerusalem! If Solomon had died when the Temple was finished! So we are tempted to say in the case of Gideon. If Gideon had only died on the field of that grand victory over Midian, then his name would have come down to us without a stain. But God knows best. You can never tell by the brightness of the dawn or the noontide how the evening of the day will be. The brightest sun may go down in a dark and clouded sky.

When Gideon came back from the rout of the foe, the liberated people, beside themselves with joy, said to him, "Rule thou over us, both thou, and thy son, and thy son's son also: for thou hast delivered us from the hand of the Midian." But sober, sensible Gideon said, "I will not rule over you, ... the Lord shall rule over you." There we could wish that Gideon had passed from the stage. Yet had he done so, though better for his fame, it would not have been better for the final lesson of his life and career.

The Midianites all wore golden earrings and anklets and chains. In a glittering heap the people piled these spoils up before Gideon. All he asked for his services was these golden earrings and chains—not for himself, but that out of them he might make an ephod, a priestly garment, whereby he might inquire of the Lord. The people willingly gave their consent. What would they not give to the nation's redeemer? But the thing became a snare to Israel and to Gideon. He assumed the prerogatives of the priest, and of the holy house at Shiloh. Instead of a shrine, that ephod became an idol, and all Israel went a whoring after it. Think of it! Gideon, the chopper, the feller, the hewer down of idols, the man who commenced his great career by chopping down Baal's grove and idol, now ends that career by leading Israel back to idolatry.

The sacred chronicler is careful to tell us that Gideon set up that ephod in his own city, *"even in Ophrah."* Ophrah, where the angel of the Lord called him; Ophrah, the scene of the great sign, when the flame rose out of the rock and consumed the offering; Ophrah, the place of his early consecration, and where there was born within his breast the purpose to deliver his people; Ophrah, where the angel had told him to destroy the dumb idol in his father's house; Ophrah, where the fleece was wet and the ground dry! One would think he would have set that ephod up anywhere in the world save at Ophrah!

What about your Ophrah, the place of your early consecration, and where heaven and earth were bright with God's glory? What will some men think when they go back to the old church and sit in the old family pew, and contrast the man of to-day, stained with the sins of the world, with the innocent youth of yesterday, with his dreams and hopes? What will some husbands and wives think when they come back to the church altar where they were made one, and where they pledged their mutual troth and love and tenderness, until death should them part? What now do they think when they stand there and contrast that early, ardent love with their present indifference, estrangement, and, perhaps, infidelity? And what does this man think when he goes back to the reunion of his college class and contrasts his lofty ambition, his pure ideals, with the present standards of his life, and looks upon the brass shields which he has substituted for shields of gold? Yes; beware of falling at Ophrah! Oh, these abandoned, forgotten, sinned-against Ophrahs of our past! Now the fleece is dry; no flame goes up from the altar; no voice of God makes the heart beat quick and the eye look up!

"Count no man happy until he is dead," the ancients used to say. But we say, "Count no man safe until the end." Ships may be wrecked at the harbor's mouth, and the day that rose in splendor may go down in darkness.

> The grey-haired saint may fall at last;
>   The surest guide a wanderer prove;
> Death only binds us fast
>   To the bright shore of love.[2]

"Let him that thinketh he standeth take heed lest he fall!" May God keep us all safe unto the end!

[2] From *The Christian Year,* by John Keble.

XII

THE NIGHT OF AGONY

"Being in an agony."

LUKE 22:44

"BEING IN AN AGONY!" TODAY THERE ARE MANY souls whose biography for the day can be written in those four words, "Being in an agony." Tomorrow there will be many more souls who will be in "an agony"; and yesterday, too, there were souls in agony. Always souls in agony! That is part of life. It is not strange, then, that he who came to redeem and rescue man should have been, at this midnight hour in the Garden of Gethsemane, in an agony. Unless Christ had been in an agony he would not have been qualified to become our Saviour. But it behooved him to be made in all things like unto his brethren. And if he was going to be made in all things like unto his brethren, he had to enter into his agony. Having been in an agony himself, he is able now to help others who have entered into their agony. Having suffered himself, and having been tempted and tried—and in the agony of this night the fearful climax of all his trials—he is able to succor and help all those who suffer and are tried. No one of us can miss his own Gethsemane.

[165]

Down shadowy lanes, across strange streams
Bridged over by our broken dreams;
Behind the misty caps of years,
Beyond the great salt fount of tears,
The garden lies. Strive as you may,
You cannot miss it in your way.
All paths that have been, or shall be,
Pass somewhere through Gethsemane.

All those who journey, soon or late,
Must pass within the garden's gate;
Must kneel alone in darkness there,
And battle with some fierce despair.
God pity those who cannot say,
"Not mine but thine," who only pray,
"Let this cup pass," and cannot see
The *purpose* in Gethsemane.[1]

When Jesus was in his agony in Gethsemane
there appeared a great angel from heaven to
strengthen him. I wonder who that angel was?
Was that high distinction given to Gabriel, who came
to tell the Virgin of the Saviour's birth? Or, perhaps, was it one of those angels who came to minister unto him after the devil had departed from
him in the wilderness at the time of his first Temptation? Jesus had asked the three disciples to watch
with him and to strengthen him in his agony; but
when they failed, and slumbered while he agonized,

[1] From "Gethsemane," in *Poems of Power*, by Ella Wheeler
Wilcox. Used by permission of W. B. Conkey Company,
publishers.

God passed their great opportunity over to an angel who did not fail him.

. . . . Before the Throne
Stands the great Angel of the Agony,
The same who strengthen'd Him, what time He knelt
Lone in that garden shade, bedew'd with blood.
That angel best can plead with Him for all
Tormented souls, the dying and the dead.[2]

Jesus in his agony had the help of that great Angel of the Agony. But you and I have an even greater Angel, the greatest Angel of them all—the Angel of the Lord, Christ himself, who trod the dark path of Gethsemane, and now is able to help every soul who enters into his agony.

'Tis midnight; and on Olive's brow
    The star is dimmed that lately shone:
'Tis midnight; in the garden now,
    The suffering Saviour prays alone.[3]

Let us follow in the footsteps of our Lord on this darkest and greatest of all the nights of his life. In the Upper Chamber the Supper is over. The sublime intercessory prayer is ended. The echoes of the hymn which he led the disciples in singing are still floating on the midnight air as we follow the

[2] From "Dream of Gerontius," by John Henry Newman.
[3] William B. Tappan.

Saviour across the darkly flowing Kedron and up the slope to the ancient Garden where he was wont to pray.

Here at the gateway of the Garden we come upon eight of his disciples. As we look about we can recognize each one of them—Andrew, Bartholomew, James the son of Alphaeus, Matthew, Philip, Simon the Zealot, Thaddeus, and Thomas. But Judas, where is he? He has just received the thirty pieces of silver for which he had covenanted with the high priest and the scribes and Pharisees to lead them to the secret rendezvous of Jesus; and even now, over yonder in dark Jerusalem, the procession is starting with Judas at the head.

We ask these eight disciples, Where are the other three—Peter and James and John? And they tell us, as we might have supposed, that Jesus had taken those three with him into the midst of the Garden. Walking under the branches of the venerable olive trees, with their shadows falling across the ground in the mean light, we come at length upon the three disciples, Peter and James and John. And they are asleep! Asleep when their Saviour has entered into his agony! These three so highly honored of Jesus, who had been taken with him into the chamber of death when he raised the daughter of Jairus, and who had seen him transfigured in glory on the mount! And all of them asleep! James and John, the sons of thunder, who had asked for seats at his right hand and his left! And Peter, who had boasted scarce an hour ago that he would never forsake him nor deny him! And, perhaps strangest of all, John, who had leaned on his breast at the Supper! How could he sleep? No one ever lived, even the most thoughtful and tender, who did not regret, when the beloved was gone, some lack of ministry, something done or something left undone, and who would not have given his all to have the dead back again, even for a moment. But for them, as for these sleeping disciples, the sentence is, "Sleep on now, and take your rest."

There is a very old and very impressive story of a youth greatly beloved who had died. In the next life he besought the gods to let him return to this world for just one day, and that day was to be one of the least notable and most ordinary days of his past life. The gods granted his request, and he appeared again just as he had been at the age of fifteen, and in his old home. As he entered the living room his mother passed him, engaged upon some household task. Then he stepped out into the yard, and his father, busy with some work and carrying tools in his hand, gave him an indifferent glance and passed on. Then the youth awoke to the fact that we are all dead, and that we are only really alive when we are conscious of the treasure we have in our friends and loved ones. A piercing parable of truth! And if that is so, that we are only really alive when we are conscious of our treasures, then how often we are dead.

But where is the Master of those three sleeping disciples? Hark! What sound is that we hear coming to us out of the distant shadows? It is the cry of a soul in anguish. Following the sound, at the distance of a stone's cast we come at length upon the Saviour himself. In utter solitude now, treading his winepress alone, there he lies prostrate on his face, the drops of blood distilling from his brow, and from his anguished lips is wrung the prayer, "O my Father, if it be possible, let this cup pass from me: nevertheless not as I will, but as thou wilt."

In silent awe we hear his words and watch his solitary struggle. At length he rises to his feet and goes back to the place where he left his disciples. Finding them asleep, he says to them, "What, could ye not watch with me one hour? Watch and pray, that ye enter not into temptation." Then he leaves them and goes off again that stone's cast, and, falling down once more on the ground already crimsoned with his bloody sweat, utters the cry, "O my Father, if this cup may not pass away from me, except I drink it, thy will be done." Then a second time he goes back to his disciples, and finding them again asleep rouses them and warns them the second time. A third time he goes back to the place of his agony and, again falling on his face, utters his cry to heaven. But this time when he rises to his feet the agony is over; the battle has been won. For his obedience and fidelity a great angel from heaven has strengthened him. On his face now, although the marks of agony are still there, there is the look of calm and courage and triumph. This time when he awakens the sleeping disciples he says, "Behold, the hour is at hand, and the Son of man is betrayed into the hands of sinners. Rise, let us be going: behold, he is at hand that doth betray me." Now he is ready for his cup. Now his word is no longer, "If it be possible, let this cup pass from me," but rather, "The cup which my Father hath given me, shall I not drink it?" Now he is ready to drink his cup, to endure the Cross and despise the shame.

He entered into his agony. How will mortal man ever explain that? Perhaps it is not possible or necessary for us to explain it; but it is possible and it is necessary for us to feel it. What was that agony into which Christ entered that night? Let us see, first of all, what it was *not*.

It was not the agony and the cup of physical suffering from which Christ shrank. The Cross was a method of punishment and death invented by a cruel people, designed not only to inflict death, but to inflict it with the greatest possible degree of torture; nor did it fail of its end. The sufferings of Christ on the Cross were terrible, for he had a perfect body as well as a true and reasonable soul. Had it been only his physical sufferings of which he had been thinking, still Christ might have said, "Behold, and see if there be any sorrow like unto my sorrow." But it was not the cup of mortal pain. Had it been that, then there would have been some ground for the complaint of Celsus, and others, that Christ on this night, and the next day on the Cross, showed less fortitude than other men have displayed in battle or at the stake.

The cup of Christ's agony was not the cup of shame and obloquy. The Cross today surmounts the temples of our holy faith; it is the symbol of all that is sacred and holy. But when Christ died upon the Cross it was the "cursed tree," the symbol of shame and degradation—so much so, indeed, that Rome would not suffer that one of her citizens should die on the cross. But Christ died on the "cursed tree"; and as if to complete the shame of it, they crucified him between two thieves. "He was numbered with the trangressors." Yet this was not the cup from which Christ prayed to be delivered.

Neither was it the cup of human hatred and anger. Bitter indeed was that cup, and more bitter to Christ than to any other, because greater was his love for

[172]

men. Well could he say, "Reproach hath broken my heart." "They hated me without a cause." Over his head on the cross was to break the most fearful storm of hatred and execration that the world has ever seen, or will ever see again. If for no other reason than that, well might the sun have veiled his face and shut his glories in when Christ drank the cup of man's hatred and reviling. But that was not the cup of agony from which he shrank.

Neither was it the cup of impending treason, denial, and desertion on the part of his friends. One can take a blow from an enemy. It is the blow from a friend that hurts. As the Psalmist of old put it, "It was not an enemy that reproached me; then I could have borne it: neither was it he that hated me. . . . . But it was thou, a man mine equal, my guide, and mine acquaintance." Already that night Christ had tasted the cup of betrayal by Judas. In a short time he was to taste the yet more bitter cup of Peter's loud and profane denial; and that night, as he had said they would, all his disciples deserted him and fled. But that was not the cup of his agony. It was not that contemplated experience that wrung the prayer from his lips, "If it be possible," or that stained the soil under the olive tree with his bloody sweat.

Then what was the cup? What was the agony into which our Lord entered? The angels and archangels themselves could not tell us all that was in that cup; and before the mystery of Christ's atoning sufferings and death they veil their faces, crying, "Holy, holy, holy, Lord God Almighty!" What we *do* know is what Christ tells us, and the Holy Spirit tells us in the Scriptures, that those sufferings which brought Christ to such an agony were for us. He was bearing our sins. He was experiencing for us the shame and the guilt of sin. He was tasting death for every one of us. He was drinking our cup. He was being wounded for our transgressions and bruised for our iniquities. He was doing that something that had to be done before the sinner can be forgiven and reconciled to God. You say you do not understand how or why that could be? Neither do I. Neither did the disciples. Perhaps the angels themselves do not understand, for Peter declared that even the angels desire to look into it. But what we can do is to accept it, to believe in it, to trust in it, and to live by it.

> We may not know, we cannot tell,
>   What pains He had to bear;
> But we believe it was for us
>   He hung and suffered there.
>
> He died that we might be forgiven,
>   He died to make us good,
> That we might go at last to heaven,
>   Saved by His precious blood.[4]

[4] Cecil F. Alexander.

It was for you, for me, that Christ entered into his agony. Does that mean nothing to you? It was for your sins and for your salvation that he drank this cup. Can you tonight see him hanging on the Tree for you? It was for you that he despised the shame and endured the Cross. When you realize that, when you realize that it was for you that he drank the sinners' cup, then in repentance and faith and love you can say as John Newton did, when he at length came to realize that it was for him that Christ had died:

> I saw one hanging on a tree,
>   In agonies and blood,
> Who fixed his languid eyes on me,
>   As near his cross I stood.
>
> Sure, never to my latest breath
>   Can I forget that look;
> It seemed to charge me with his death,
>   Though not a word he spoke. . . . .
>
> A second look he gave, which said:
>   "I freely all forgive;
> This blood is for thy ransom paid;
>   I die that thou mayst live."

XIII

THE NIGHT A MAN FOUGHT AN ANGEL

"And Jacob was left alone; and there wrestled a man with him until the breaking of the day."

GENESIS 32:24

THIS, UNDOUBTEDLY, IS ONE OF THE GREATEST nights of the Bible; but it is also one of the most mysterious, one of the most difficult to explain. Time and time again I have come up in my studies of the Bible and the characters of the Bible to this night when Jacob wrestled with the angel, and never yet with much satisfaction have I set down my conclusions concerning it. Nor have I ever read any exposition of this narrative which has helped me a great deal. Nevertheless, the drawing power, the fascination, of this story of the midnight encounter with the angel is irresistible. There are a few great truths here which we can bring out, even if we cannot penetrate to the heart of this battle of Jacob, for it has all the mystery, and yet all the fascination of the night.

Let us recall the events which led up to this midnight battle. After twenty years of toil and perse-

verance which had been crowned with success, Jacob
is coming back from Padan-aram and the home of
Laban to his own country. He had gone out with
nothing but his staff; but now he comes back a rich
man, with flocks and herds, and his two wives and
their children. On the way back, at Mahanaim,
angels of God met him. With all his worldly, grasp-
ing nature, and ofttimes sensual indulgences, Jacob
saw a great deal of the angels, and with his dying
breath he testified to how the angel of God had led
him. At this particular time he sorely needed the
visit of those angels at Mahanaim, for as he drew
near to his own country there rose up before him
to frighten him and dismay him the memory of his
old transgression. He remembered how he had
cheated his brother Esau and got from their father
the blessing which belonged to the older brother.
Fearful of the vengeance of Esau, Jacob seeks to
placate him and sound him out with a present. But
the only answer that he gets is that Esau with four
hundred men is coming to meet him.

In his great distress, Jacob, after having divided
his flocks and herds into two caravans, so that if
Esau should fall on one the other would escape,
prayed earnestly to God, saying that he was not
worthy of the least of all the mercies that God had
bestowed upon him, and asked God to deliver him
from the hand of Esau, his brother.

SIN FINDS YOU OUT

Here, at least, whatever mystery shrouds the events of this night, is one truth, one fact which stands out clearly; and that is the fact of retribution, the fact that we must meet our sin. "Be sure your sin will find you out." Jacob might have hoped that twenty years would have dulled the memory of his transgression in the mind of Esau. But whatever had happened to Esau, Jacob's sin had a swift and terrible resurrection within his own breast. As the golden sunset fades and the shadows gather over the desert and the stars come out, Jacob is afraid, for he must face himself.

"Be sure your sin will find you out." There are many things in life that you cannot be sure of. You cannot be sure of where you will be a year from today, or where you will be tomorrow night. You cannot be sure about your companions, your place, your work, your life. But here is one thing that is sure, fixed, certain, immovable, and that is that *your* sin will find you out. There are three ways in which sin finds you out. First of all, it finds a man out in Time. The general tendency of evil-doing is to uncover and discover itself to the world. All officers of justice, all investigators of crime, avail themselves of this great truth, that the tendency of sin is to come to the surface. "Murder will out." Sin finds a man out in Time.

The second way in which sin finds a man out is in Conscience. It is conceivable that a man might be able to hide in the recesses of his own bosom— although that it very difficult—his dishonesty, his licentiousness, or other transgressions; but he cannot do it in his conscience. This is the truth that is brought out in Thomas Hood's great poem, "The Dream of Eugene Aram." Aram, an usher at a boys' school in England, had committed a murder. One day he was in charge of the boys on the playing field. Seeing a boy reading a book under a tree, the usher asked him what he was reading. The boy answered, "It is 'The Death of Abel.'" The usher then sat down by the boy and told him how he had dreamed that he had murdered an innocent old man, robbed him of his gold, and then flung his body into the river. When he went back at dawn he saw the body lying on the river bed, the stream having dried up. Taking it out of the river, he buried it under the leaves in the forest, only to see the wind uncover the corpse by sweeping the leaves away. The frightened boy listened to the usher in amazement. That very night Eugene Aram was carried off in gyves to prison. But as he was sitting on the playing field that day, he closed the book that he was holding, "strained the dusky covers close, and fixed the brazen hasp," exclaiming as he did so:

> Oh, God, could I so close my mind,
> And clasp it with a clasp!

But that is impossible. You cannot close the mind and clasp it with a clasp. Conscience keeps the book of transgression forever open.

The third way in which sin finds a man out is in Eternity. We must all stand before the Judgment Seat of Christ and give an account of the deeds done in the body. Here, for a time at least, perhaps a man might be able to hide his sin from others; and here, for a time at least, in the business and pleasures of the world, a man might cease to hear the accusing voice of conscience. But in the Judgment there is no evasion and no escape.

Having sent his caravan across the river before him, and having provided as best he could for his family and his wives, and especially for the beloved Rachel, Jacob, held by some mysterious power, remained by himself on the eastward side of the Jabbok. And as he waited in anxiety, in fear, and in agitation, suddenly he found himself in desperate combat with one whom he could hardly see and could not name. All through the night Jacob and his antagonist struggled to and fro under the trees on the banks of the river. At length, when the day was about to break, Jacob's adversary touched the hollow of his thigh and put it out of joint. Now Jacob was helpless—that is, helpless so far as he could hope to conquer this antagonist who had gripped him in a contest. But he could still cling to him. He could still hold to him. He had some dim realization now that this was no ordinary midnight assailant with whom he was contending; certainly he was not Esau, whose vengeance he had feared; and when his antagonist said to him, "Let me go, for the day breaketh," Jacob answered, "I will not let thee go, except thou bless me!" Then the angel, for angel it was who was wrestling with him, said to Jacob, "What is thy name?" Jacob had to confess that his name was the crafty one, the supplanter, Jacob. Then the angel said, "Thy name shall be called no more Jacob, but Israel: for as a prince hast thou power with God and with men, and hast prevailed." And there the angel blessed Jacob. And when the sun was risen and the angel had departed, Jacob, realizing the great change that had come over him, called the name of that place "Peniel: for I have seen God face to face."

THE BLESSINGS OF ADVERSITY

Out of that sublime but mysterious narrative we gather now a second truth, and that is that ofttimes the adversaries against whom we struggle, and who struggle against us, are really angels in disguise. Jacob found that out that night. He struggled desperately against this mysterious battler, fearing for

his own life, and striving with all his might to overcome him and destroy him. But by the end of the
night he made the discovery that this mysterious one
was not really an enemy, but an angel who had power
to bless him, and he determined to get that blessing.

At the fourth watch of the night—the darkest
and most fearsome watch, just before the dawn—
on that stormy night on the Sea of Galilee, after
the disciples had been battling for so many hours
with the tempest, toiling at the rowing because the
wind was contrary, when they saw Jesus walking on
the sea towards them they thought he was a ghost and
cried out in terror. But in a moment they heard his
voice as he said, "Be of good cheer; it is I; be not
afraid!" Then they knew that it was Jesus, and all
their fear departed from them. So some of the
providences of God will seem to you when first
they come upon you to be specters, enemies, ghosts—
anything but a friend. But God is in them and his
love is in them, just as Jesus was in the storm that
night on the Sea of Galilee.

When Jacob realized that this midnight battler
with whom he had been struggling had the power
to bless his life, he clung desperately to him and
said, "I will not let thee go, except thou bless me."
Are you in the midst of any trouble, or any sorrow,
or any trial or heartache? Then this is my word
for you: Offer the prayer of Jacob that night on

the banks of the Jabbok, "I will not let thee go, except thou bless me."

GOD IS THE GREAT DISCOVERY

The great fact and the great truth of this midnight struggle by the ford of the Jabbok is that Jacob that night discovered God, and that discovery changed the character of Jacob. Hitherto he had heard of God with the hearing of the ears, but now his eye saw him. Now God was a reality to Jacob. It was that discovery of God which made the change in Jacob, and which merited that change in name from Jacob, the stealer and supplanter, to Israel, one who has power with God, a prince with God. What honor on earth, quickly fading, is to be compared with that—the honor of being a prince with God!

Whittaker, the pilot of the bomber in which Rickenbacker and the seven men came down on the lonely Pacific, in his moving narrative of that great odyssey of the sea, says that what he saw and experienced on that terrible voyage, the preservation of their lives in answer to their prayers, first by the capture of the sea gull which landed on Rickenbacker's head, and then by the superhuman power that was given him to row the raft in which he and his two companions lay against the strong offshore current to safety and deliverance on the coral island, had changed him from an atheist to a believer, from an infidel to a Christian, to one who henceforth, all his days, in his thoughts and in his words and in his deeds, would try to thank God and to honor him. He said, "I have made the greatest discovery that a man can make. I discovered God."

Yes, that is the greatest discovery that any of us can make. And whether it be made in a rubber raft on the vast expanse of the Pacific, with sharks circling about you and death staring you in the face, or in the quiet of your home or study, or in the midst of the day's business, or on a Sabbath evening in a church, blessed is the man who makes the discovery! "Blessed is the man whose God is the Lord!" Have you made that discovery? Have you found God through faith in Jesus Christ his only Son?

XIV

THE NIGHT OF THE GREATEST QUESTION

"And at midnight Paul and Silas prayed, and sang praises unto God: and the prisoners heard them. And suddenly there was a great earthquake."

ACTS 16:25-26

TO THE NORTH RISES A RIDGE OF HILLS; TO THE south an immense barrier of the Macedonian mountains; in between is the vast plain where, one hundred and ten years before, the mastery of the world had been settled when the ghost of Julius Caesar overtook Brutus.

On this plain lies the sleeping city of Philippi; but in the jail men are not sleeping. Hush! What sounds are these that we hear coming through the iron-barred window of the prison? Men have sung before in prison, but they have been songs of obscenity and cursing and intoxication, the shouts of despair, and the groans of the transgressor, the shriek of the prostitute, and the maledictions of the criminal. But here is a different kind of music. Two prisoners in this jail, their arms and their feet in the stocks, and their backs bleeding from the brutal scourging of the Roman magistrates, are singing praises unto God.

It would have been a great thing to have heard Paul preach, to have stood near him when he preached to the philosophers on Mars Hill, or in the governor's palace at Caesarea when Felix trembled at his preaching and Agrippa cried out, "Almost thou persuadest me to be a Christian!" But still more I would like to have heard Paul sing, for when a man sings there is an expression of his soul which no other utterance can give. What if you could hear a voice on the radio saying, "This is Station Alpha and Omega, Philippi, Macedonia, St. Luke speaking. Stand by! In a moment you will hear Paul and Silas sing!"

Listen! You will hear some of the songs that the soul still sings when it is in prison. "Yea, though I walk through the valley of the shadow of death, I will fear no evil: for thou art with me." "I will bless the Lord at all times." "God is our refuge and strength." "He hath looked down from the height of his sanctuary; from heaven did the Lord behold the earth; to hear the groaning of the prisoner; to loose those that are appointed to death." "When thou passest through the waters, I will be with thee; and through the rivers, they shall not overflow."

These were the old, old songs that rang out at

that midnight hour in the Philippian dungeon; and
as Paul and Silas sang, all the prisoners heard them
singing. I suppose their singing was answered at
first with profane jests and ribald laughter. The
child stealer from Ephesus said, "What angels are
these who have come to our prison?" The robber
and bandit from the Egnatian Highway said, "They
sing now, but by morning they will have learned our
language and pitch their voices to another tune."
The murderer from Thessalonica said with an oath,
"If this right arm of mine were free from the stocks,
and these two feet of mine, I would smash in their
teeth with my fist and put an end to their singing."

But the apostles sang on. A hush of silence and
wonder fell over the prisoners in that dark and dismal dungeon. Tears stole down cheeks which had
long been strangers to them. Thoughts of innocence
and long-forgotten happiness came back to those
hardened criminals, and many a heart grew soft
with the recollection of yesterday, and from many
a breast came a sigh which was dangerously near to
a prayer.

> Down in the human heart,
> Crushed by the tempter,
> Feelings lie buried that grace can restore.[1]

The prisoners heard them singing. The prisoners

[1] Fanny J. Crosby.

listened and were moved, because they too had in them the capacity for songs like that divine song. Every man has within his heart a chord which, although silent now, can be awakened into divine melody. We can almost feel the hush and silence of those other prisoners as they listened to Paul and Silas singing.

The prisoners heard them singing. Paul and Silas were singing primarily for their own comfort and hope; but as they were singing all the other prisoners heard them. As you go through life, remember that on the other side of the wall, on the other side of the street, in the room or office next to you or above you, there are others who will hear you if you sing the song and lead the life of Christian faith and hope. What do life's prisoners hear from you as you pass by? When the Pilgrim was passing through the Valley of the Shadow of Death, in Bunyan's immortal allegory, he was so dismayed at the fearful sights and sounds that he heard, the flames and the demons, that he was on the point of turning back. But just then, out of the smoke and darkness ahead of him, he heard a voice saying, "Yea, though I walk through the valley of the shadow of death, I will fear no evil: for thou art with me." At that the Pilgrim took new heart and courage and pressed on through the dreadful valley. Some of your best influences as you go through life will be your unconscious influences. Men you have never known may rejoice because one day they heard you sing.

That was the greatest prayer meeting, the greatest song service ever held, and it received the greatest recogntion on the part of God, for suddenly, at midnight, there was a great earthquake which shook the foundation of the prison, laid its walls flat, and loosed every prisoner from the stocks. The jailer, awakened out of his sleep, and seeing that the prison doors were open, took it for granted that the prisoners had escaped, and drew his sword, intending to fall upon it. When prisoners escaped, Rome held the life of the jailer forfeit. This jailer preferred to fall on his own sword rather than wait for the vengeance of Rome. But Paul, seeing what he had in mind, cried out, "Do thyself no harm: for we are all here." When the jailer heard that, amazed to discover that his prisoners had not fled, he cried out, "What must I do to be saved?"

THERE IS SOMETHING TO BE SAVED FROM

"What must I do to be saved?" Saved from what? Not the earthquake, for it was over. The earth was again terra firma. The terrible tremors of the earthquake were past. Not from the judgment of Rome, for the prisoners were all there.

None had escaped. No, it was something else than the earthquake shock or the judgment of Caesar that this jailer had in mind. His question, undoubtedly, had to do with his soul, with his relationship to God. In some way there had been brought home the conviction that all was not right between him and God, that he needed salvation, and that these two Hebrew prisoners, with their ankles and wrists swollen from the stocks, and their backs still raw and bleeding from the cruel scourging which he had inflicted upon them, knew the secret and could tell him what he must do to be saved. And they told him! "Believe on the Lord Jesus Christ, and thou shalt be saved."

It is important to remember what Paul did *not* say to this man. He did not tell him there was no occasion for alarm. He did not say to him, "Sir, do not be alarmed. There is no danger. There is nothing from which you need to be saved. The earthquake and the exciting events of this night have upset your nerves. Calm yourself, Sir, and forget your question." A strange answer, you might say; and yet not so strange after all, because if you look about you in life you see many living as if that were the real answer. Surrounded by automobiles, radios, pleasures, a mass of things, they live out their lives as if they themselves were only another kind of thing. But this jailer knew that he had a soul, and through the Holy Spirit there had come to him the conviction that he was a sinner, and that the wages of sin is death, and that he needed a Saviour.

Again, Paul did not tell this jailer that he could save himself. He did not say to him that night, "You have been a cruel and rapacious jailer, extorting bribes from your prisoners, beating them, abusing them, and starving them. Let the tragic events of this night, this earthquake, teach you a lesson. Change your ways. Repent! Refrain from evil; deal justly henceforth with your prisoners, and all will be well." There are many today who are living on the principle that they can save themselves. They are citizens of what John Bunyan called the Town of Morality. Their reliance is upon their own life, and not upon the life of Christ offered up for them on the Cross. They may not claim any perfection, only that they have lived fairly decent, upright lives; and as for sins and transgressions and shortcomings, a merciful God will overlook that. But that is not the way of Salvation, and that is not the answer that Paul gave to the Philippian jailer at that midnight hour when the walls of the prison had fallen down. He did not tell him that he could save himself; but he told him the true and only way: "Believe on the Lord Jesus Christ, and thou shalt be saved."

SALVATION BY FAITH ALONE IN CHRIST

Great changes have come over the world since those words were spoken on the midnight air to the Philippian jailer. But Paul's answer is still the great answer. Let us try to see what it means.

There are different kinds of faith. We speak of faith in one another, faith in the laws of the universe, faith in the future of America, faith that the Allied Nations will win the war. Still higher is faith in God: that he exists, that he created the world, and that he upholds it and us by his power and providence. Still higher is faith in Christ; that is, to the extent, at least, that Christ lived and died and rose again and that he was the Son of God; in other words, that the great facts related of him in the Scriptures are true. But this is not evangelical, scriptural, saving faith. What the New Testament means, first of all, when it speaks of faith in Christ, is the reliance of a soul upon Christ for salvation. It is faith in what Christ did for you and me as sinners upon the Cross—that by his death we are reconciled unto God and have pardon and eternal life. One of the greatest definitions of Faith ever made is that of the Shorter Catechism— and remember it was made by some man who knew that he was a sinner and had found Christ as a Saviour—"Faith in Jesus Christ is a saving grace whereby we receive and rest upon him alone for our salvation."

In my mother's church, Great Hamilton Street in Glasgow, there was a young theological student who served as the church missionary. Afterwards he went out as a missionary to the South Sea islands. In the newspapers you read of our airmen, shot down in those southern seas, managing to land on one of those islands. Instead of beating in their brains and boiling them in a pot and devouring them, the natives treat them with great kindness and hospitality. That change is largely due to the fact that the young missionary, John G. Paton, brought to those islands the knowledge of Christ and the Christian way of life. When he was at work translating the Scriptures into the language of those natives, John G. Paton was at a loss to discover the equivalent in their speech for the word "faith," and without that word the translation of the Bible would be in vain. Day after day he listened to the speech of the natives, hoping that he might hit upon some expression that would represent what the Bible means by faith. But months passed and the word was still wanting, until one day a native came into his study and, throwing himself down upon a chair, exclaimed, "How good it is to lean my whole weight upon this chair!" The missionary caught at that expression, "lean my whole weight upon." There

was the word for which he had been searching!
There was the word for belief and faith, and never
was a better one used. Saving faith in Christ is
"leaning your whole weight upon him" for salvation.

The supreme illustration of what faith is, and how
it saves, is Christ's own illustration of the Brazen
Serpent: "As Moses lifted up the serpent in the
wilderness, even so must the Son of man be lifted
up: that whosoever believeth in him should not perish, but have eternal life." This was the event in
the history of Israel from which Christ drew his
illustration. For their rebellion and unbelief and
murmuring God had sent serpents into the camp of
Israel, and the people were dying of the bite of the
serpents. At the direction of God, Moses set up
in the midst of the camp a pole with a brazen serpent entwined about it. Then he spake the Word of
the Lord to the people, telling them that whosoever
looked upon that brazen serpent would not perish.
If they looked in obedience and faith their lives
would be spared. That brazen serpent, and their
look of faith, was God's plan for saving the people
alive. "Even so," said Christ, "must the Son of
man be lifted up: that whosoever believeth in him
should not perish, but have eternal life."

When Paul then said to this Philippian jailer, "Believe on the Lord Jesus Christ, and thou shalt be

saved," he meant that the jailer was to put his trust upon Christ and him crucified. That is the only way of salvation. John said he wrote his gospel that men might believe that Jesus was the Christ, the Son of God, and that, believing, they might have life through his name. "There is none other name under heaven given among men, whereby we must be saved." Could God have chosen some other way to save men, some other way which would satisfy Divine Justice, and at the same time show God's infinite love and mercy? We judge from the Scriptures that he could not, that even God is limited as to a plan of salvation. But whether God could have saved in any other way or not, this is his appointed way of salvation.

It is a way of salvation in which Christ takes the hard part. He bore the Cross, the sin, the shame, the agony. It is a way of salvation that humbles man and exalts God, for we are saved not through what we ourselves have done, but by what Christ did for us on the Cross.

It is a way of salvation which produces a godly life in the man who accepts it. This jailer was saved through his faith in Christ; but as soon as he became a believer, he brought forth his good works and showed his faith by his works, for in the same night this converted and redeemed jailer took Paul and Silas and washed their wounds and stripes.

[195]

Wherever a man's faith in salvation centers upon the Cross of Christ, there you can be sure you will see the fruits of the Spirit and the fruits of the Christian life.

Finally, this is a way of salvation that honors and exalts Jesus Christ. God not only planned to save men, but to save men in a way which shall glorify and exalt his Son Jesus Christ. Christ is exalted as the Creator of the world. He is exalted as Judge of the world. He is exalted in the praise and homage of the angels, the cherubim and the seraphim. But, most of all, Christ is exalted in the salvation of sinners through faith in his Cross.

What is a man saved to? He is saved to himself. He is saved to the fellowship of just men made perfect. He is saved to the Kingdom of God. He is saved to what Paul calls "glory and honour and immortality." He is saved to all that glory and peace and joy which God had in mind for man when at the beginning the Triune God said with himself, "Let us make man in our image." To know all, or perhaps even a small part, of what that means we shall have to wait, I suppose, until we get to heaven ourselves, and join Paul and Silas, and that converted jailer, and the whole company of the Redeemed, as they sing their songs of grateful praise "unto him that loved us, and washed us from our sins in his own blood."

XV

THE NIGHT OF THE GHOST

"He walked on the water."
MATTHEW 14:29

ANYBODY CAN WALK ON THE LAND. THAT IS EASY. The land is man's natural element. But the test is, Can you walk on the sea? Can you walk on the sea of your tribulation and sorrow? Can you walk on the stormy waves of your temptation? Can you walk on the sea of your disappointment or loneliness or affliction?

The sad word had come to Jesus and the disciples of the death of John the Baptist, who had been murdered by Herod to please his vindictive paramour, Herodias; for John had denounced Herod and Herodias for their adultery. When John's disciples had buried his body—although his spirit could never be buried—they went and told Jesus. As soon as Jesus heard the word, he called his disciples together and, getting into a boat, withdrew to a desert place across the Sea of Galilee. That was the fitting tribute Jesus paid to his great forerunner, John the Baptist. Jesus had declared John to be the greatest man that had been born of woman, and in all his dealings with him and his references to him

[197]

he treated him with the highest deference and re-spect. When he hears that John is dead, that he is a martyr to conscience and to the Kingdom of God, Jesus stops his own preaching and healing for a season and withdraws to a desert place. He paid John the Baptist a tribute of silence and solitude.

The death of our friends deserves the tribute of silence and solitude. If once it was a custom for people to go to the extreme in their mourning for those who had passed out of life, today it would seem to me that many have gone to the other ex-treme, and that far too little deference and respect is paid to the event of death and the passing of our friends. Silence and solitude, for a season at least, fit such an occasion.

If you were to take the Sea of Galilee out of the Holy Land, its most pleasing physical feature would be gone. And if you were to take the Sea of Gali-lee out of the narratives of the four Gospels, much of their charm and beauty would be gone. On the shores of that sea Jesus wrought some of his most memorable miracles, such as the healing of the cen-turion's servant and the woman with the issue of blood, the raising of the daughter of Jairus, the feeding of the five thousand, the healing of the wild man of Gadara; and on two occasions he quelled the tempest on the sea. The traveler wandering on the lonely shores of that beautiful sea finds it far easier to think of his Saviour and come near to him in spirit than he does in the narrow streets of Nazareth or in the noisy and crowded streets of Jerusalem.

The multitude had gone along the shore of the lake and were waiting for Christ when he arrived on the other side. Night was coming on, and the disciples advised Jesus to send them into the villages that they might buy food for themselves. But Jesus said unto them, "They need not depart." What a world of meaning is poured into that sentence of Christ: "They need not depart." Great are the resources of Jesus. From him none ever needs to depart. You need never leave him for some other philosophy or way of living or way of salvation. He was sufficient that evening for the physical needs of five thousand people. He is sufficient for all your needs. In any time of sorrow, or temptation, or trial, or loss, or pain, remember these words of Jesus: "They need not depart."

After he had fed the multitude, Jesus dismissed them. Then, having compelled the disciples, evidently against their wish, to get into the boat by themselves and start across the lake to the other side, he climbed a mountain in order that he might be alone in prayer. There you can see him climbing higher and higher up the side of the mountain, perhaps pausing now and then to turn and look at the disciples' ship as it was beginning to fade and disappear on the distant horizon. If we are going to follow in the footsteps of Christ, we must remember that, and have our own periods when we are alone. The dread of solitude is a source of weakness. No great discovery was ever made on a crowded street, but in the quiet place of retirement. Sublime thoughts never rose in the mind of one in the midst of the shouting thousands. It is when man goes apart into the desert place, or climbs the mountain as Jesus did on this night, that his best thoughts and purposes are born and his soul is fortified with strength. One of the most impressive things in the eighty-eight-year-long life of John Wesley was when he was taken with his last illness. He returned from the house of a friend where he had preached his last sermon, on the text, "Seek ye the Lord while he may be found." His friends and housekeeper carried him up to his chamber adjoining the City Road Chapel. Realizing that his end was not far off, the aged saint desired all his friends and his servants to leave him for one half hour by himself. Obedient to his desire, they all went out and left him, and there John Wesley met his God alone, reviewed the incidents of his long life, and prepared for death.

THE STORMS OF LIFE

When the disciples started out on their journey across the sea that night, all was calm and fair. The sea was peaceful; the wind was soft and gentle; and the stars were beginning to come out. But by the time they were halfway across the sea, a hurricane broke over the ship. Peter, no doubt, took command; and you can see him there holding the tiller with his stalwart arm, and his beard anointed with the foam of the sea, as in stentorian tones he commands the disciples to trim the ship, lower the sails, and take to the oars. Where all was calm a little while ago, now all is tumult and confusion. As the tempest rages over the lake, the ship tosses like a cork up and down in the great waves, the white foam of the great rollers gleaming in the blackness of the night like the teeth of some monster of the sea.

Life has its storms. Like the start of the disciples that night, the start of life's voyage is generally calm, and with favorable winds; but ere long the gentle winds change to contrary winds, and the hurricane rages. "The wind was contrary." These winds are sure to smite the ship. Here a storm broke over those who were in the path of duty. A storm broke over Jonah's ship, and that seemed fitting and appropriate; for Jonah was fleeing from the face of the Lord and was sailing for Tarshish instead of for Nineveh, where he had been commanded to go. But here the storm breaks over the disciples who have obeyed the command of Jesus. Storms come in the path of duty, too. How many contrary winds there are that blow—winds that smite the body, or the mind, or the spirit; winds of sorrow, or remorse, or sickness, or fear, or discouragement. But however contrary the wind may be, it can never blow without God's permission.

In his graphic account of this storm Mark writes, "And when even was come, the ship was in the midst of the sea, and he alone on the land. And he saw them toiling in rowing; for the wind was contrary unto them." He saw them "toiling in rowing"! From his mountain outlook he could see now and then in the flashes of the lightning the black speck of their ship as it tossed up and down on the waves. Christ always knows when you are toiling at the rowing. The disciples, no doubt, wondered why Christ had sent them out into the storm, and yet more, why he did not come to them and still the tempest. Perhaps they were tempted to feel that he had forsaken them. But Jesus saw them toiling at the rowing. When the wind is contrary and the rowing on life's sea is hard, Christ always knows it.

Recently I received a letter from a woman who had suffered greatly through the death of a much-beloved father. With his dying breath he had enjoined her to be sure to care for her sister, a helpless blind girl. This she has done with great fidelity. Yet she is conscious of a great loneliness. What she asked was, "Does God really care? Can we count upon the sympathy of Christ?" It just happened that I had been reading from Mark's Gospel the story of this storm on the Sea of Galilee. So my answer was right at hand. She wanted to know if she could count on the sympathy of God. I told her to read the story of this miracle, and especially this verse, "The ship was in the midst of the sea, and he alone on the land. And he saw them toiling in rowing; for the wind was contrary unto them." Yes, we can always count on the knowledge and sympathy of Christ. "There is no place where earth's sorrows are more felt than up in heaven."

He saw them toiling at the rowing, and yet he delayed to come unto them. Hour after hour he let them struggle on in the midst of the hurricane, wondering why he did not come to help them. These delays are a part of God's plan of operation in the world. Ages passed after the fall of man before the Saviour came to redeem us. Thirty years of his life on earth passed before he began to preach in the power of the Holy Spirit. When Mary and Martha sent word to him, "He whom thou lovest is sick," he waited three days before he started for Bethany, and when he arrived there Lazarus was dead. On his way to heal the daughter of Jairus, he stopped on the street of Capernaum to talk with a woman who had touched the hem of his garment, and by the time he started again for the ruler's house, his daughter was dead. Expect, then, what may seem to you a delay in the coming of Christ. Yet these delays are not incompatible with his knowledge and sympathy. Why did he wait that night so long to go to the rescue of the disciples struggling with the waves and the wind? I do not know. Perhaps he wanted to wait until all hope had been given up, that their extremity might be his opportunity to teach them his power and revive their faith. But that is mere conjecture. You cannot always know why God waits; but you can always know that God cares. He sees you toiling at the rowing.

THE GHOST

At length he came to them, sometime during the fourth watch—that is, between three and the dawning, that time when human energies are at their lowest, and when it is easy to yield to fears and despair. Now he comes to them. But his coming at first seemed worse than his delay.

There are the disciples in the ship, holding on desperately to thwarts or gunwale or mast, as the ship plunges in the waves. Peter is holding the tiller. Suddenly he cries out, "Look! What is that?" By the tone of his voice, which rose louder than the winds and the waves, the other disciples knew that it was something terrible that Peter had seen. Looking off over the waves they saw a ghost, a specter, striding across the sea towards them. In their terror they cried out aloud; literally, they "shrieked."

That was not strange. That other hidden world has never lost its power over this world, in spite of all our rationalism and infidelity and unbelief. A ghost is something that we read about in old books, or see on the stage, knowing, of course, that it is not a ghost. But if you really believed that a ghost, a disembodied spirit, a messenger from the world of the dead, was actually here, walking down the aisle of the church, you would cry out as the disciples did that night and flee from the church. The disciples cried out in terror when they saw Jesus walking on the sea towards them. They thought he was a ghost, a water demon, coming to sink them and send them to the bottom. First they thought they were going to perish in the storm. Now something worse than the storm was coming down on them—a ghost! They were fishermen, and they could fight against the storm; but what could they do against a ghost?

Often in our troubles God's providence appears to us something other than it really is. As Jesus seemed a specter to the disciples that night, so God's providence at first may seem to us harsh. And yet it was in the storm that night that they found and

[205]

knew Christ as they had never known him before.
It was darkest for them just before the dawn.

CHRIST STILLS THE TEMPEST

In their terror the disciples were almost ready to
leap into the sea, rather than face that ghost. Then
suddenly they heard a voice: "Be of good cheer; it
is I; be not afraid." How glad they must have been
when they heard that voice! What they saw was not
a demon, nor a water fiend who had come to send
them to the bottom of the sea; for the voice was
that of their Friend and Master, so calm, so un-
afraid, so kind, so reassuring, just as they had heard
it so many times before. The moment they heard
his voice, the raging sea lost its terror and they no
longer feared the ghost. Instead of trying to row
away in terror from the approaching demon, the
disciples rested on their oars and received Christ
into the ship; "and immediately the ship was at the
land whither they went." That is John's poetic way
of putting it. Mark says, "And he went up unto
them into the ship; and the wind ceased." And
Matthew says, "And when they were come into the
ship, the wind ceased."

What is your contrary wind? What is your
storm? Storms are sure to come; but remember how
Jesus came walking that night on the sea to his
disciples in their terror and fear, and how, when they

had received him into the ship, the wind ceased and the storm was over. Is your storm some hurt of the heart or soul? Receive him into your ship. Is your storm some fear or anxiety or worry? Receive him into your ship. Is your storm some hatred or enmity? Receive him into your ship. Is your storm some discouragement or despair? Receive him into your ship. Is your storm some loneliness of soul? Receive him into your ship, and you will have the Companion who never leaves you nor forsakes you. Is your storm some temptation or besetting sin, or some bitter memory of past sin? Then receive him into your ship; for he can say to its angry winds and waves, "Be still." Will you receive him into your ship? Will you receive him now? Immediately?

PETER WALKS ON THE SEA

We have three stirring accounts of the storm that night on Galilee, and how Jesus came to his disciples. But Matthew adds a paragraph of his own, which is not only of intense interest, but of great profit to our souls.

As soon as the disciples heard the voice of Jesus saying, "Be of good cheer; it is I; be not afraid," and their fear was turned into joy, Peter called out over the waves, "Lord, if it be thou, bid me come unto thee on the water." That was just like Peter, was it not? In his exuberant enthusiasm and joy he cannot wait for Jesus to come to the ship so that he can welcome him, but he wants to go to him himself. He feels, too, that he would like to walk on the sea like his Master. And he is convinced that he can do it. When he said, "If it be thou," he did not mean that he had any doubt about it; but it was as if he had said, "Since it is thou, and since thou hast dominion over all things, bid me that I come unto thee on the sea."

And Jesus said to him, "Come!" He was pleased with Peter's enthusiasm and daring. He is pleased when he sees us ready to dare great things and to venture all for our faith in him. So he said to Peter, "Come!" And Peter went. He stepped over the edge of the vessel into the sea and walked on it. There you can see him, striding over the waves with his eager gaze fixed upon Christ. What a picture that is of triumphant faith! But Peter's miracle and victory were short-lived. After a little, hearing the roar of the wind and seeing the foam of the great waves breaking about him, Peter became frightened and began to sink. He had looked at the winds and the waves and looked away from Christ, and that moment he began to sink.

How true that is! When we forget Christ, when we look away from him, then all we see is our peril, our danger, our foes, our adversaries, our own weakness, our sins, and we begin to go down. When he saw the wind was boisterous, he was afraid and began to sink. Yet in that brief experience Peter told us a great truth. We *can* walk on the sea. Christ invites us to do so. He bids us come to him on the angry waters of life; and even when our faith falters and we begin to sink, he is there to stretch out his hand and deliver us as he did Peter that night.

THE CHRIST OF FLANDERS

Balzac has a great tale, suggested perhaps by an ancient legend of Flanders, but also undoubtedly suggested by this story of Peter walking on the sea. One evening long ago the ferryboat was about to start from the island of Cadzant, off the coast of Flanders, to Ostend on the mainland. The passengers were all aboard. Night was coming on, and the skipper of the ship, before undoing the iron chain which held his boat to a stone at the quay, blew a warning blast on his horn to call any late-comer. Just then a man appeared as if from no-where and boarded the boat. He was bareheaded; his garments had no ornament; and there was neither purse nor rapier at his girdle.

In the better seats at the stern of the ship were seven persons of the higher class: a cavalier, with his gilded spurs and curled mustache and jewel-bedecked cap; a proud damsel, with a falcon on her wrist; her mother and an ecclesiastic of high rank; a fat merchant from Bruges; and a doctor of science from the University of Louvain, with his clerk. The moment they saw the advent of the latecomer, they hastened to sit down, so as to prevent him from taking a seat in their midst.

The stranger gave a swift look at the stern. Seeing that there was no room or welcome for him there, he went forward to the bow of the ship, where the poor and the plain people were gathered. These were a young working woman with her little child; an old soldier; a poor wrinkled and ragged old woman, who in her youth had been a prostitute, and now sat crouched on a coil of rope; and a peasant with his ten-year-old son. As soon as the stranger came among them, the old soldier and the young mother moved along and made room for him. Then the skipper blew his horn for the last time, and the ship was off on its journey for Ostend.

But the vessel had not gone far when the sea and the sky took on an ominous look and gave forth warning sounds and groans and murmurs, as of an anger that would not be appeased. In a moment a hurricane broke over them. Suddenly the clouds parted for a little above the vessel, and in that transient light all the passengers looked with amazement at the aspect of the latecomer. His golden hair, parted in the middle on his tranquil, serene forehead, fell in many curls on his shoulders, and outlined against the gray sky was a face sublime in its gentleness and radiant with divine love.

Meanwhile all the passengers were in fear for their lives as the ship plunged in the storm. The young mother cried out, "Oh, my poor child, my child, who will save my child?" "You yourself," replied the stranger. And when the mother heard his sweet voice, she had hope in her heart. The rich merchant, falling on his knees, cried out, "Holy Virgin of Perpetual Succor, who art at Antwerp, I promise you twenty pounds of wax and a statue if you will get me out of this." But the stranger spoke, "The Virgin is in heaven." The handsome young cavalier put his arm around the proud damsel and assured her that he could swim, and that he would save her. Her mother was on her knees asking for absolution from the bishop, who was blessing the waves and ordering them to be calm, but was thinking only of his concubine at Ostend. The ragged old prostitute cried out, "Oh, if I could only hear the voice of the priest saying to me, 'Your sins are forgiven you,' I could believe him." The stranger turned towards her and said, "Have faith, and you will be saved."

When the ship, almost in view of Ostend, driven back by the convulsion of the storm, began to sink, the stranger stood up and walked with firm steps on the waves, saying as he did so, "Those that have faith shall be saved. Let them follow me." At once the young mother took up her child in her arms and walked with him on the sea. Then followed the soldier, and the old prostitute, and the two peasants. And last of all came one of the sailors, Thomas, whose faith wavered, and who sank several times into the sea; but after three failures he walked with the rest of them. The merchant went down with his gold. The man of science, who had mocked, was swallowed up by the sea. The damsel and her lover, the bishop and the old lady went to the bottom, heavy with their sins. But those who had faith followed the stranger and trod with firm, dry feet on the raging waters. At length they reached the shore, and the stranger led them to a fisherman's cabin, where a light flickered in the window. When they had all come in and were gathered about the fire, then the Saviour disappeared.

"Those that have faith, let them follow me!" Can you walk on the sea? Anyone can walk on the land; but can you walk on the sea? What is your sea? Is it a sea of sickness? Is it a sea of loneliness? Is it a sea of disappointment? Is it a sea of pain? Is it a sea of sorrow? Is it a sea of temptation? You can walk on it if you will. Will you make Peter's prayer, "Bid me come unto thee on the water"?

XVI

NIGHT NO MORE

"And there shall be no night there."
REVELATION 22:5

A REDEEMED SOUL, RECENTLY ARRIVED IN HEAVEN, received a commission from one of the great arch-angels to go forth on a mission of power and grace for Almighty God. Heaven will be more than a vast rest house. There they go from strength to strength, and great occupations will be linked with perfect intelligence and perfect power. The re-deemed soul heard with delight the great task which had been assigned to him, and, having received his final instructions, said to the archangel, "The sun is already high in the heavens, and I must hasten and be off on my great undertaking, lest night should overtake me before I return, and the twelve pearled gates of the city be closed against me." But the archangel looked upon him with kind benignance in his countenance and said, "Spirit, you have forgotten. You are in the land now where there is no more night, and where the gates of the city shall not be shut at all by day, for there shall be no night there."

"Night no more!" We have traveled through the Bible by night. We have turned away from the glare of the garish day and have walked in the shadows of the night and listened to the mysterious voices of the night. By night we saw Egypt doomed and Israel delivered. By night we saw the angels climb the ladder of Jacob's dream, and by night we saw Jacob struggling with an angel on the ford of the Jabbok. By night we read the handwriting on the wall and saw Belshazzar slain amid his drunken revelers. By night we heard the roaring of the lions and saw Daniel delivered out of their mouth for his loyalty to God. By night we heard Peter go out and weep bitterly. By night we saw King Saul enter into the cave of the Witch of Endor and hear the doom that Samuel pronounced upon him. By night we saw Paul's ship crash on the rocks of Malta. By night we heard the crash of the earthquake at Philippi and saw the jailer come into the Kingdom of God. By night we saw the shepherds kneeling in adoration and heard the chorus of the angels when Jesus was born at Bethlehem. By night we saw Jesus walk upon the sea, and by night we saw him still the tempest. By night we saw our Saviour kneel in his agony in Gethsemane and heard him pray, "If it be possible, let this cup pass from me!" By night we saw Judas receive the sop into his traitorous hands and go out into the night that knows no morning.

But now we have finished with the Night. We

have come to an end of all these nights of the Bible, and to an end of Night itself. "There shall be no night there." That is the last, the final thing, and the crowning thing, that is spoken of heaven. We are told of its Sea of Glass mingled with Fire; of its great White Throne; of the rainbow round about the Throne; of the four and twenty elders; of the Seven Spirits of God; of the Hallelujah Chorus and the New Song of Moses and the Lamb; of the sounding trumpets and the hundred forty and four thousand; of the streets of pure gold; of the Twelve Gates that were twelve pearls; of the foundations of the wall, garnished with all manner of precious stones; of the pure River of Water of Life, and on either side of the River the Tree of Life, which bare twelve manner of fruits. But here is the final, conclusive, and all-embracing thing that is said about the heavenly city and the heavenly life: "There shall be no night there!"

Why is it that we know so little about the life to come? Why is it that Jesus, who knew all about heaven, said, after all, so little about it? The full answer must wait, I suppose, until we arrive in heaven, when the night of our ignorance will be over. But no doubt we have received as much revelation and knowledge about the life to come as in our present state we are able to receive. After his experience in heaven and his vision of it, Paul said that he heard and saw things which it is not lawful for man to utter—meaning, perhaps, that it was impossible for him to explain it to those who had not had a like experience. He had no language with which to tell it. Furthermore, it must be true that more knowledge about heaven would not comfort us or warn us more than our present knowledge does. Jesus said that if a man came out of the future life, out of that part of the world to come which is reserved for the punishment of condemned souls, his preaching and warning would have no greater effect upon men in this world than the knowledge they already possessed. Likewise, if one were to come to us from heaven and speak of its ineffable joys, its great enterprises, its resounding music, his message would not comfort us and inspire us any more than our present knowledge.

It is an interesting fact that some of the chief things we are told about heaven are in the negative, what is *not* there. If you were going to describe to an untutored savage of the arctic regions some rich tropical country, you could hardly give him a conception of it by mentioning the things that are there. What would palm trees mean to a man who had never seen anything but arctic berries and snow and ice? What would the flash of brilliantly plumaged birds mean to one who had never seen any bird but the gull or penguin? What would an elephant or lion mean to him who had seen only the floundering seal? You would have to begin the other way. You would have to begin by telling him what was not there—no snow, no ice, no polar bears. In a way, that is the method the Holy Spirit employs in telling us about the life beyond the grave. It tells us, first of all, what is *not* there—things to which we are accustomed here, which we shall never see and never experience there.

Of all these negative descriptions, the most beautiful, the most satisfying, and the one which sums up and includes all the other negative descriptions, is that there shall be no night there. To the weary earth night comes down with the benediction of peace and silence and rest. But when the Bible says there shall be no night there, it means night as the symbol of unrest, and ignorance, and distress, and darkness. When the sailors on Paul's ship had cast those four anchors out of the stern of the vessel to hold her off the rocks of Malta, Luke says that the soldiers and officers and passengers and prisoners, as they huddled together on the deck of that vessel as it pitched in the waves, "wished for the day." After all, that wish sums up the history of mankind. What is the history of man but a deep, pathetic longing and wishing for the day, when the dark shadows shall disappear and the light shall come? And now at length has come the fadeless morning.

They that sat in darkness now behold the light which shall not go out.

Let us look at some of these negative descriptions of heaven which, after all, are also positive, and answer every desire, known and unknown, of the human heart. The best way to take them and to hear them is to put this glorious final description of heaven before each one of them, for if there is no night there, it is because the shadows which are cast by these things in human life have disappeared.

First of all, there shall be no night there because there shall be no pain there. Pain in this life is the great enigma, even when we realize that pain is in some way linked with the catastrophe that has overtaken human nature, and that it has penal and disciplinary and probationary purposes, and that it can refine the spirit. Still, pain remains a great mystery. It raises deep questions as to God and his administration of the world. The natural and involuntary expression and ejaculation of those who are in intense pain, of those soldiers who are dying for us in the air, or on the battlefield, or on the blazing deck of the battleship, is "O God!" Pain makes men think of God. It makes men appeal to God. Pain, indeed, may be a minister and surgeon of God. But who, passing down the corridors of pain in this world, and hearing the cry of mortal agony, has not wished that he had the power to put an end to pain and smooth the furrow from the ruffled brow of agony. What we wish for here will be the reality of the heavenly life. No shadow shall fall over man, and over man's thought of God, because in that land there shall be no more night of pain. There shall be no more pain.

Again, there shall be no night there, for there shall be no more night of sorrow. "God shall wipe away all tears from their eyes." Sorrow and pain lie very close together. Sometimes sorrow is the result of pain. But there is a deeper pain than that of the body. There is the pain of the spirit and the pain of the heart. How wonderful a thing is the human heart, and how great its capacity for sorrow! What if Christ had been known to us only as the Man of Joy? Then he never could have been our Saviour. He had to be touched with the feeling for our infirmities; and when he assumed human nature he became the Man of Sorrows, for sorrow is one of the deepest facts of human life. When we hear that Jesus wept, then we are willing to listen to him. His most tender moments on earth were when he wiped away the tears of those who wept— that woman who washed his feet with her tears, the tears of Mary and Martha, and the tears of Mary of Magdala at the sepulcher.

Through the whole creation rolls the deep dirge of human sorrow. In that dirge I hear the cry of the little child, of the strong man in the midst of his years, and of the aged also. When you see someone in tears—a little child that is lost, or a mother weeping over the child she has lost, or a man weeping like Peter over his sins and transgressions—who has not wished that he had the power to wipe away all tears from his eyes? Alas, that can never be here in this world, a world that rightly man has called the Vale of Tears. But yonder it will be so. What could be more beautiful, and what more tender, than that word that is spoken concerning the heavenly life, "And God shall wipe away all tears from their eyes"?

"There shall be no more curse." This is the same as saying, "There shall be no more sin," for the curse is nothing but the curse of sin. Sin and curse are used interchangeably in the Bible. Wherever there is a curse there has been a sin. Wherever there is a sin there has been a curse. That is true ever since the curse fell upon man after his sin and fall in the Garden of Eden. The old hymn by Isaac Watts has it:

> He comes to make His blessings flow
> Far as the curse is found.

But where is the curse not found? Where is sin not found? The dark shadow of sin falls everywhere across the world. Sin is as universal as human nature and as eternal as human history. But now the long reign of sin is ended. Sin is so common a fact in our present life that it is almost impossible for us to imagine a world without the shadow and the curse of sin. What a world this would be if there were no sin in it! What churches, what cities, what schools, what homes, what nations, if there were no more sin, no more guilt, greed, lust, envy, hatred, jealousy, lying, cruelty!

With their beautiful and poetical descriptions, the ancient prophets, in those Messianic passages sketching the millennial bliss, delight in extending the peace and good will of that day even to the brute creation: "The wolf also shall dwell with the lamb, and the leopard shall lie down with the kid; . . . . and a little child shall lead them. . . . . And the sucking child shall play on the hole of the asp, and the weaned child shall put his hand on the cockatrice' den. They shall not hurt nor destroy in all my holy mountain: for the earth shall be full of the knowledge of the Lord, as the waters cover the sea." The whole creation lies thus in the sunshine of God's favor and peace because sin and its curse have vanished. In magnificent but prophetic triumph, Paul cried out, "O death, where is thy sting? O grave, where is thy victory?" Here we can say that only in faith, only in contemplation, only in view of the promised fruit of Christ's great victory over sin upon the Cross. But when we arrive in heaven and when we promenade together down those great avenues, and see the river of Water of Life, clear as crystal, and the flashing of those gates of pearl, and listen to the music of ten thousand times ten thousand, that I think will be the ejaculation, the expression, most frequently upon our lips: "O death, where is thy sting? O grave, where is thy victory?" Now we know what that means. Now we have arrived in that country where there shall be no more night of sin.

Finally, there shall be no more night of death. How long a reign death has had! But now that reign is ended. The Rider on the Pale Horse, who from the dawn of creation has gone forth with hell in his train, and with authority to kill with the sword, with famine, and by the wild beasts of the earth, he himself is now unhorsed by the White Horse and his Rider. The King of Terrors himself is uncrowned! There shall be no more night, for there shall be no more night of death.

Our meditation on the heavenly life, with which we bring these night journeys to a close, will be in vain unless we try to reflect some of that heavenly light on the path we take through this world, and to create some of that heavenly life in our own lives and in the lives of others. Another rendering of Paul's great illuminating sentence, "We shall also

bear the image of the heavenly," is, "Let us also bear
the image of the heavenly." The thought seems to
be that even now, as yet bearing the image of the
earthly, we can illuminate and transform that image
and that earthly life with the heavenly image and
the heavenly life. How grand a thought that is! I
have known some, and no doubt you have known
some, who were so brave, so pure, so forgiving, so
kind, that even here and now they seemed to bear the
image of the heavenly. By the help of Christ, you
too can bear the image of the heavenly. Do you
wish that heavenly light to shine out from your life
even here, now?

Sometimes we wonder what the friends on the
other side would say to us if they were permitted to
bring messages to us. I am sure they would have
wonderful things to tell us. To those whose hearts
are broken and who walk in sorrow, they would
bring the message not to mourn as those who have no
hope. They would tell their friends here on this
side that the souls of the righteous are in the Hand
of God, that they drink deep from the river of God's
peace and happiness and joy which proceeds out of
the throne of God. To those on this side who doubt,
they would bring the message of faith in the life
to come, how that life is more wonderful than has
ever entered into the mind of man. To those who
are tempted, they would say, "Endure every loss,

suffer every hardship rather than consent to sin, for that is the one great tragedy." To those who have sinned and gone astray, they would bring the message of pity and pardon. To those who are without Christ and without hope, they would bring the message of repentance and faith in the Lord Jesus Christ, and of immediate repentance while it is still called today, and ere the night cometh. They would say that it is on this side, and on this side only, that men can repent and believe in Christ. They would say that the only bridge by which we can cross from this life to the blessed life of heaven is that Cross upon which the Saviour died. Yes! That is what our friends on the other side would say to us if they could speak to us now. Hark! I hear their voices, and some of them are speaking your name. They are God's messengers to you. Will you hear them and obey them, now?